BANK & BROKERAGE
BACK OFFICE
PROCEDURES &
SETTLEMENTS

Mervyn J. King

Glenlake Publishing Company, Ltd.
Chicago • London • New Delhi

AMACOM
American Management Association
New York • Atlanta • Boston • Chicago • Kansas City • San Francisco • Washington, D.C.
Brussels • Mexico City • Tokyo • Toronto

© 2000 Mervyn J. King
All rights reserved.
Printed in the United States of America.

ISBN: 0-8144-0534-7

Printing number

10   9   8   7   6   5   4   3   2   1

CONTENTS

Contents

Contents

Appendices

PREFACE

Just how much money has been lost owing to misdirected payments, inefficient management of funds, inaccurate processing, fraud, collusion across all instruments, markets and geographical locations? Does the name Orange County mean anything to you? Have you ever heard of Barings and Nick Leeson? Where were you when BCCI went bust?

Was there ever any danger in dealing with a bank which was one of the 50 largest in the world? Then who was it who caught the biggest cold when LTCM's problems arose? Were not UBS and Bankers Trust involved? Of course, just like contracting a terminal illness or being involved in a road/train/plane accident, it will never happen to you. Want to bet?

From Cinderella to belle of the ball, from necessary evil to board favourite, from an ill-defined philosophy to a science - that has been the history of the back office/settlements function. What has brought about this metamorphosis - the size of the markets, technology, fall-out from past errors or flexibility brought about by the arrival of new instruments?

Why *Back Office and Beyond*? - because the original concept of a back office and its duties was the starting point which has now been extended far 'beyond' its original scope and function. The 'beyond' factor entails not just the changed role regarding processing and payment but also presages the additional requirements now for aspects of risk management to be sited within the back office area. Indeed back office is intrinsically involved at first base; for if all data is not captured accurately in the first instance, there is little chance of the eventual output, in respect of the institution's risk profile, being accurate.

Already plans are having to be made to incorporate the implications of a single currency in Europe, which again will heavily involve the back office functions. Indeed, it could open up further opportunities for an institution to 'steal a march' on its competitors. The later chapters of this book will explore these developments.

Life began with just a few currencies which traded in small volume at almost fixed levels, where foreign exchange equated to trade only. Now it has evolved to a multi-faceted market where size and speed of movement has opened up Pandora's box - if not controlled quickly, efficiently and intelligently. Now the demand is for all the full implications of risk across its broadest interpretation - risk regarding position/counterparty/correlation to other markets, etc.

On the one hand interaction between markets and volume has increased, whereas the onus for wide-ranging experience/knowledge in processing (ie, not front office) has become heavily compartmentalised and reduced to a single figure evaluation - value at risk (VaR).

How did it all begin? Where are we today? What rules are there? How much interpretation is allowed? How many fixed reference points are there? Had it been left solely to the central banks to cover each variation, then little would probably have been achieved. We only have to look at their inaction at the time of the oil price rises in the 1970s, and the resulting fall-out in the market when commercial loans to emerging countries were not repaid, or the Plaza Agreement and Louvre Accord over-reactions, to judge their contribution. However, there is no real point in citing the problems created by government or their agents when, at the end of the day, timely, accurate and efficient settlement of all trades is the overall goal.

Purpose of this book

Since there is no fixed one and only way in which trades can be settled, the purpose is to establish, where possible, those few fixed reference points and what is generally accepted as 'best practice' whilst also identifying some 'caveats' of the pitfalls to look out for, using actual historical events and practical examples.

Despite considerable polarisation of market roles over the last three to five years *vis-à-vis* the percentage of transactions spread between an ever-decreasing number of principals, every institution still needs to be able to settle its own trades. Thus, whatever their position in the batting order, for example, as identified annually by *Euromoney* - there is a prerequisite for all transactions initiated by front office to be processed by back office without any loss of income - apart from those accepted as shared universally between departments for funding of accounts and ancillary charges.

Thus there has been an exponential change in the responsibility level of back office reflecting that same change in the front office though, via specialisation, the demands for speedy settlement have resulted in fragmentation of responsibility, knowledge and authority with little understanding of respective roles. Pressure can restrict progress! TRAX on bond settlements (see page 37) requires a trade to be entered within 30 minutes of execution; transaction automatic matching (TRAM) via the automated time out management system (ATOM) function (see Appendix 3) imposes time-outs for unreconciled items; individual currency cut-off times make their own demands. With so many banks offering the same products at similar pricing (more and more relevant as the market consolidates/contracts) this means that the one thing that distinguishes one bank from another is the level and quality of service provided to its customers and other banks.

The move to control risk via netting implies simultaneous release of net amounts receivable/payable but does not actually demand it and VaR figures can only be produced once back office has input all transactions.

How does this all occur? I have naturally approached this exercise from a UK point of view since the UK, London and the Bank of England have been in the forefront of most developments, whether from the front or back office perspective, and remain so today and will be for the future the prime source for 'best practice'.

Market ethics and codes of behaviour have always been better than average in London and it is well known that London's practices are constantly being emulated in the rest of the world, even to the extent that the regular updates of the European Monetary Union (EMU) from the Bank of England are acknowledged as the most professional and thorough and an example to all those central banks which will actually form the core of the first wave of members in 1999.

Obviously, every centre has its own local flavour to its regulatory set-up, but the basics that have been identified for this book will not vary significantly from the UK base. Read on......

CHAPTER 1

III

IN THE BEGINNING...

One of the many concerns arising from the advances in information technology, financial innovation, deregulation and intensified competition has been the vast growth in the volume and value of financial transactions across the world's payments and settlements systems. (See Bank for International Settlement (BIS) survey results on page 114.) In the UK alone some £120 billion of settlements occur daily of which about half is constituted by the sterling settlement of foreign exchange transactions. Additionally about the same amount (£120 billion) is settled daily representing money market, gilt-edged and equity payments. If one extrapolates the figure for global operations, then in foreign exchange alone some $2 trillion exchange hands each day.

It will easily be appreciated therefore that as these numbers have increased there has been a commensurate increase in the payment and settlement risk implicit within them. The risk that, after having settled - or at least sent the payment instructions - the sold/lending side of the transaction or the receivable amount due is either received late or not at all.

Every bank/institution relies upon the receipt of funds in order to be confident of being able to honour other commitments. Any payments/settlement failure could have very serious consequences upon the whole payments system - not just in the local currency but on a global scale. Such a catastrophe would be capable of creating a complete 'gridlock' on the global payments system - given the degree of interdependence - with a resultant inestimable effect upon trust/creditworthiness.

Obviously there have been changes, which in most cases are consistent with improvements but, although the ultimate funds transfer may be handled via computers, the instructions are generated by a human being who is fallible. Thus the efficiency and reliability of the back office staff and their appreciation of the risks of the operations of the front office is paramount. Similarly, the attention given to the training of this vital area and its ability to keep up with the developments of both instruments and systems will single out some institutions from others with whom counterparties will be willing to trade rather than others. Furthermore, as further rationalisation takes place in both the number of institutions being actively involved in the financial markets and the instruments traded have less liquidity, the back office could assume even greater importance, as institutions vie for the available business.

The list of 'near misses' and general concern regarding the size and impact of mistakes and fraud on the vast sums involved has led to central banks being involved in encouraging banks and computer companies to come out with new/efficient controls and in establishing some of their own recommendations on minimum acceptable levels of control. As ever, however, the onus for action has remained with the commercial banks.

History

Passing reference was made in the Preface to the historical evolution of the markets leading to the requirements today of the modern efficient back office. Although history does seem to repeat itself, it is not the purpose of this book to trace back the history of front office: back office relationships beyond 1946.

Why 1946? At that point the United States dollar (USD) was established as the numeraire for world trade and became the currency in which most transactions were expressed, commodities were priced and reserves were held (see Tables 1.1 and 1.2).

Given that the USD was replacing the now less relevant, and economically fraught, Great Britain pound (GBP) the major currency in which transactions took place was GBP/USD/ Cable. (As price in those days was transmitted via the cable that went under the Atlantic Ocean). At this stage, however, the size of trade was small (still recovering after the Second World War) and thus individual transaction size, the spread in the price and the speed of delivery were all extremely different to those of today.

Table 1.1 World's reserves by currency (source: Dresdner Bank).

	USD billions 1975	%	USD billions 1985	%	USD billions 1994	%
USD	124	76.8	203	53.0	555	48.9
DEM	9	5.8	51	13.2	183	16.1
JPY	1	0.7	26	6.9	102	9.0
GBP	6	3.6	10	2.6	21	2.8
CHF	2	1.4	8	2.0	14	1.3
ECU	0	0.0	42	10.9	80	7.1
Other	19	11.6	44	11.5	168	14.8
Total	**162**	**100**	**383**	**100**	**1,134**	**100**

The effects of the depredations of the war, the size of world trade at that time and the less exiguous demands regarding settlement were not the only influencing factors. At that stage, the actual number of currencies that were tradable were far smaller as were the number of active trading centres and principals involved - ie, no huge flows from mutual funds (Soros/Paul Tudor, etc) and cross-boundary investment in bonds or stocks. Also the state of technology had a lever effect on the status, relevance and efficiency of any so-called 'settlement' function.

What has been experienced since that time has passed through:

- Simple foreign exchange (FX) and money market (MM)
    Spot and forward up to one year
    Fixed deposits

- More currencies/instruments
    Forward up to five years
    Capital market instruments

Table 1.2 Official foreign exchange reserves by region (sources: IMF, national data and BIS).

	1994	1995	1996	1997	Amounts outstanding at end 1997 in billions of US dollars
	Changes, at current exchange rates				
Total	153.0	200.1	172.3	45.9	1,578.5
Industrial countries	60.9	79.3	69.6	-10.3	692.6
Asian NIEs[1]	31.7	22.7	17.5	-4.1	272.2
Other countries	60.4	98.1	85.2	60.3	613.7
	Changes, at constant exchange rates[2]				
Total	112.2	182.1	200.6	105.3	1,578.5
Dollar reserves held	90.7	143.8	161.8	54.5	1,103.5
In the United States[3]	38.3	106.0	128.0	20.6	738.7
With banks outside the US	30.0	-15.4	19.2	-4.0	122.2
Unallocated	22.4	53.2	14.6	37.9	242.6
Non-dollar reserves	21.5	38.3	38.8	50.8	475.0
of which held with banks[4]	1.8	7.6	8.0	17.0	126.1

[1] Hong Kong, Korea, Singapore and Taiwan. [2] Partly estimated; valued at end-of-year exchange rates. The residual has been allocated on the basis of known reserves. [3]Excludes foreign military sales prepayments and the current value of zero coupon bonds issued to the governments of Argentina, Mexico and Venezuela as collateral for their Brady bonds. [4]Deposits by official monetary institutions with banks reporting to the BIS.

- Off balance sheet/ derivative markets
  FRAs
  Futures
  Swaps
  Options

All through this period of development, central banks have become more and more concerned about the operations/risks of the markets and thus become more demanding as to the reports that they receive. Their real concern has been the fear of 'systemic' risk or 'gridlock' referred to earlier, ie, the chance of the whole market coming to a standstill because of the failure of a major player in one or other market.

Systemic risk

The problems of the long term capital management (LTCM) fund could have been 1998's offering for a systemic failure. In this case it was a non-bank where concern over the lack of control compared to that imposed on banks has often been expressed. However, the impact was upon the banking system and could have had disastrous, domino effects.

The Federal Reserve organised a $5.9 billion where it saw a 50% chance that the whole US financial system might unravel. The Fed was not so much concerned with the investors who would lose several billion dollars, but with the risk that several credit and interest rate markets would experience extreme price movements and cause markets to close temporarily. This, in turn, could then have led to a general loss of investor confidence, the widening of credit spreads, more liquidations of positions and then to an interested cost of capital to American business.

LTCM lost over 50% of its capital through a misjudgement of emerging markets in which it had leveraged itself via derivative instruments up to an exposure of $100 billion. Fourteen institutions were brought together by the Fed to bail out LTCM - including some banks who had additional exposure via direct investment in LTCM.

While such an eventuality is not entirely preventable, it could have been mitigated had the requirements of reporting and management of risk, which are now in force, been in place then.

Self-regulation has been tried to back up internal controls, but lapses still occur. It is, however, more far-reaching in the financial world (ie, banking) for a number of reasons:

- The central role occupied by banks in the payments system.

- The need for confidence in what is a fragile environment running massive transfer of funds.

- The inextricability of the simultaneous inter-relationship of banks and overlapping instruments with the possibility of systemic collapse (see Figure 1.1).

Figure 1.1 Close shaves (for fuller details of some of these see March 1996 edition of BIS publication, *Settlement Risk in FX transactions*, sections 2.2.1 - 2.2.5).

Herstatt	6/74 - Buba closes bank at 10.30 - half-way through day.
Contill	1982/4 - insolvent.
Bank of New York	11/95 - computer failure threat to CHIPS system - $23 bio bail-out by Federal Reserve Bank.
Drexel Burnham Lambert	2/90 - liquidity problem; Bank of England (B of E) bail-out.
BCCI	7/91 - liquidated before paying out to UK and Japanese counterparty - fraudulent dealing.
Invasion of Kuwait	8/90 - B of E and other counterparty banks (CBs) avoided gridlock on dinar.
Soviet Coup	8/91 - counterparty banks refused to pay out to Sovie banks, even though they had paid countervalues.
Barings	2/95 - after its collapse, ECU clearing almost gridlocked.

Each of the situations cited above has led to a renewed attempt to impose further controls from without, when the original problem stemmed from within - either through lack of internal controls or failure to maintain them. The original Banking Act of 1879 might have been expected to put that right, requiring, as it did, 'every bank which registers under the act to publish at least once per year its exact financial position... and to submit their books to external auditors'. Such optimism had not anticipated the Bank of Credit & Commerce International (BCCI) scenario.

The problem with the reliance on auditors to 'do the necessary' ignores the fact that an external auditor, works for, is paid by and has his primary duty to the client, although that is now under review. Other external intervention would have to be so intrusive, pervasive and expensive as to be immediately unenforceable.

As a result the onus, responsibility (and sometimes blame) must rest with the internal controlling departments and the auditor - although there is still room for the central authorities which can calibrate the external burden of regulation by (say) the number of visits, frequency of reporting or the range of products allowed. If one refers back to the Barings case, Barings was understood to have an excellent VaR model in operation, yet it did not enforce that oldest and most vital first control - segregation of back office duties and reporting lines. Technical expertise can never offset or prevent human failings (or fraud).

This vital support role offered by back office has always been seen as a non-profit making area - front office merely depends on it not to lose the profit already made - but, considering the overall scope of the modern settlement function, it should be quite easy to appreciate that the few extra points gained in the price of the trade pale into insignificance when compared to the cost of a failed settlement.

The repercussions could be limited to a small fixed charge for an amendment to the beneficiary or date, via the more serious overdraft charge to the extreme, although not impossible situation, where a failed settlement was instrumental in a failed share purchase/company take-over/bond issue with resultant bankruptcy a strong possibility.

Enough of the generic, let's look at the specifics!

CHAPTER 2

THE SET UP AND ROLE OF BACK OFFICE

Set up

The first essential in every bank is that the dealing function is separated from the settlements function and that both have separate management reporting lines. The set-up incorporates not only the personnel, systems and hardware but also the correct relationship between the staff and duties of front and back office.

A dealer should never have the opportunity to make a payment on a deal and, conversely, settlements staff should never have an opportunity to undertake a market deal or write up a deal ticket. Therefore, the FX/MM dealing environment where the deal is initially concluded must always be separated from the settlements department where payments are made. This so called 'Chinese Wall' divides the lines of responsibility between the two departments (London Code of Conduct - p.7, s. 46/47). It follows, therefore, that reporting lines have to be strictly separated, which if not clearly established and monitored (see Figure 2.1), could result in another Barings, Singapore, case.

Co-operation is obviously a *sine qua non* but a good back office will keep on top of the front office and try to anticipate problems and plan accordingly. Mutual appreciation including knowledge of respective roles will make the difference between a growing reputation for your institution (and a participating bonus!) and a major loss of money, reputation and - maybe - your actual job!

Figure 2.1 Front office/back office reporting lines.

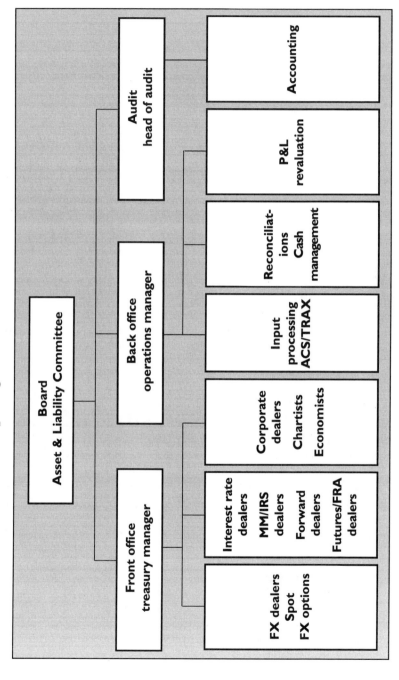

Co-operation without any undue familiarity extends to actual family/relationship ties. It is also vital that relations (brothers/sisters, husbands/wives, boyfriends/girlfriends, etc) are not employed in interdependent roles. Thus management must always be aware of any such relationships to ensure that there is no potential for collusion between a dealer and someone in the back office which could lead to trades being altered, payment instructions changed or revaluation rates being doctored.

Attention to 'system security' will assist in this area. This entails ensuring that only those authorised have access to systems or parts thereof. For example:

- Codes for releasing payments through Society for Worldwide Interbank Financial Telecommunications (SWIFT), Central de Livraison de Valeurs Mobilières (Cedel), Euroclear, etc, should be restricted to those authorised to release such payments.

- Sensitive information (eg, revaluation rates/programmes) should be either password or 'view only' protected to prevent unauthorised access/tampering.

- All staff with password protected access should be trained to sign off when away from their terminals.

In the same context, although for a different purpose, back office staff will be responsible for correct retention period for records - ie, the legal and/or 'recommended' period for retention of records varies both by law and by internal rules according to type. If insufficient attention is given to the set-up then all the roles that flow from it are at risk of failure.

The role of back office

The actual title given to the function will vary between any of the following:

- Back office.
- Back-up.
- Settlements.
- Middle office.
- Support.

Normally the justification for the specific title describing the role is dependent upon the size and role of the front office. So, whatever it is called (see Figure 2.2), what is/should be the function of this area?

The essential role covers the three main areas of reputation, risk and reward where the market forces which drove them can be summarised as in Figure 2.3.

Reputation

Any institution needs to protect its reputation in what is a most competitive market. An excellent service from the front office can all too easily be destroyed by an inefficient back office. Thus a courteous, efficient processing and follow-up operation can make all the difference. A reputation lost is not easily regained!

Risk

Risk management is very high profile in today's markets. However, the risk cannot be properly managed if the original input is either incomplete or inaccurate, which then leads to incorrect data being included in management or external reports.

Reward

Back office cannot make money, but it could quite easily dissipate profits earned by the front office. An efficient back office today has the incentive to perform to its utmost by the right to participate in front office profits. Essentially the back office role falls into two phases - physical settlement of all transactions and post-settlement functions.

Physical settlement

This entails carrying out a series of duties in respect of all transactions emanating from front office (treasury, capital markets, corporate finance, syndicated loans, etc) effectively leading to making an actual payment - in full or as part of a netting arrangement - in the right currency, in the right place and at the right time. This sounds easy, doesn't it? What on earth could go wrong?

Post-settlement

This will involve a plethora of responsibilities relating to the consequences of the processing/payment (eg, confirmations/SSIs and account maintenance) to the consequences (eg, cash management, nostro reconciliation and margin account management) and ancillary matters (eg, management reports, P&L calculations, tapes and risk).

Figure 2.2 Operations structure.

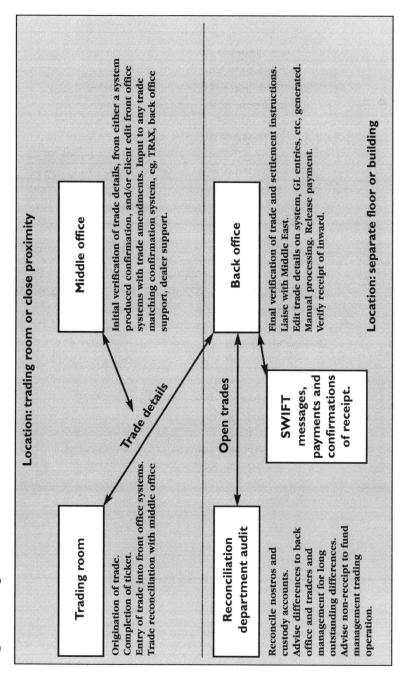

Location: trading room or close proximity

Middle office

Initial verification of trade details, from either a system produced confirmation, and/or client edit front office systems with trade amendments. Input to any trade matching confirmation system, eg, TRAX, back office support, dealer support.

Trading room

Origination of trade.
Completion of ticket.
Entry of trade into front office systems.
Trade reconciliation with middle office

Trade details

Back office

Final verification of trade and settlement instructions.
Liaise with Middle East.
Edit trade details on system, GL entries, etc, generated.
Manual processing. Release payment.
Verify receipt of inward.

Location: separate floor or building

Open trades

SWIFT messages, payments and confirmations of receipt.

Reconciliation department audit

Reconcile nostros and custody accounts.
Advise differences to back office and traders and management for long outstanding differences.
Advise non-receipt to fund management trading operation.

17

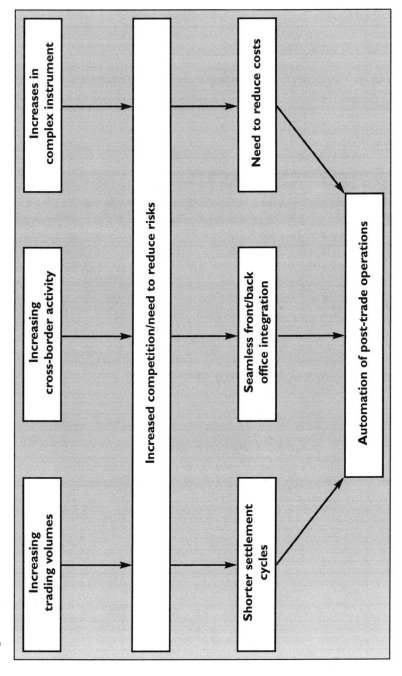

Figure 2.3 Market forces.

Let's now take this step by step.

Processing

From the moment a trade/deal is struck (see Figure 2.4), front office is only thinking of how and when to turn it into a profit - thereafter, as far as it is concerned, it has completed its involvement with that trade and all subsequent responsibility passes to the back office. Since back office will also handle internal transactions - ie, transactions between two sections of its own institution - there should be no temptation/excuse to treat such deals any differently from those with external clients. The same degree of control should be exercised whatever the source of the trade.

Figure 2.4 The FX transaction flow.

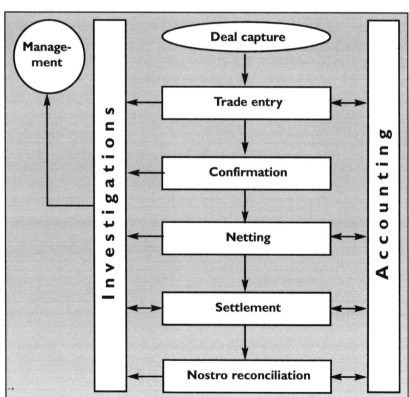

Deal completed by front office

Are the details of the deal complete? Well, what should be included? This depends, once again, on the size, mechanisation, etc, of the front office operation depending on whether the deal tickets are manually completed, partially mechanised or dealt with by straight-through processing.

Basically, the trade should have the following:

- The counterparty (bank or corporate client) with whom the host bank has traded.
- The amount and currency sold (and amount borrowed or loaned if MM deal).
- The amount and currency bought (and interest amount if MM deal).
- The exchange rate of the deal (and interest rate if MM deal).
- The value date of the deal (and maturity date if MM deal).
- The medium through which the deal was made (eg, broker/phone/Reuters/telex).

Is the deal written for the:
- correct amount?
- correct value date?
- correct counterparty - name and branch?
- correct currency pair?

Are the settlement details:
- included at all?
- in agreement with SSI?
- possible? (You cannot pay Swiss francs (CHF) to the Bank of Tokyo.)
- subject to a netting agreement?

If all is in order, then the deal can be released to the computer, the input can be checked, released to the accounts department, the pay instruction can be sent and confirmation awaited.

Not every one of these details is relevant to every type of transaction and points such as maturity, settlement amount and settlement method present a multitude of choices and potential confusion.

Wait a minute! Let's take that from the top one more time......

Manually completed tickets

Depending upon the number of individual input forms being used, some minor or major understanding of the transaction involved is required of the processing staff in order that the deal ticket is both complete and accurate. This could mean something relatively simple, in the case of Spot = 2 currencies and amounts:

- Deal date.
- Counterparty.
- Value date.
- Exchange rate.
- Intermediary (phone/European Banking System (EBS)/Reuters/broker).

An interest rate swap (IRS) needs all the above plus:

- Day basis for interest calculation.
- Interest payment basis (annual/semi-annual; money market or bond basis).
- Currency of interest payments.
- Documentation - International Swap and Derivative Association (ISDA)/British Bankers' Association Interest Rate Swap (BBAIRS)/other.
- Exchange rate (if a currency rate swap - CIRS).
- Settlement medium - Cedel/Euroclear/Fedwire, etc.

Thus these details may be missing, included but not needed and incorrect anyway.

Partially mechanised tickets

This situation occurs when either all EBS or Reuters 2000 deals have 'default' data already supplied or when some data is automatically inserted to the deal typed, for example, an internal system produces its own deal ticket from a blank format on to which all relevant data is transcribed. However, this effectively leaves back office with the need to check/make amendments to all/some deals as in a manual situation.

Straight-through processing

Here there is no need for intervention by back office in supplying and checking details and the deal passes via computer input system to automatic confirmations (TRAX/TRAM, etc) to the generation of the payment via the appropriate medium (SWIFT/Clearing House Interbank Payment System (CHIPS)/Clearing House Automated Payment System (CHAPS), etc see Appendix 3. All that is left is to release the payment.

CHAPTER 3

III

LIFE OF A DEAL

Whatever the niche of any institution and whether the deal is manual, part-ly mechanised or completed by straight-through processing, the essential elements of a deal follow the following steps.

Deal capture

Originally, the back office would have been responsible for the deal capture of all details as automised/customised front office systems did not exist. Thus, once the dealer had manually entered the basic data, the back office staff would also manually enter all other details. This would have entailed a multitude of individual records for each type of transaction plus the master card, for example:

- Spot DEM purchased
- Spot DEM sold
- Forward DEM purchased
- Forward DEM sold

One of each of these per currency per customer was required, and a master for total DEM purchased/total DEM sold.

NCR 32 machines were a favourite semi-mechanised system for this, with huge bins of cards for all the records. End of year reconciliations and then subsequent transfers to computer-based systems were a nightmare! At least at that stage there was not the plethora of instruments or the inter-related position reports required.

The duties, however, were just the same as today - accurate recording, speedy transmission of payments and reconciliation of differences were and remain essential. Any back office worth its salt would insist that its efficiency has never been in doubt, but it is worth bearing in mind that 'prevention is better than cure' - ie, it is much better to get the initial payment right, for it can be very difficult/time-consuming and costly to get a payment returned.

Front office systems

Some banks develop their own computer systems for capturing and recording the life of a deal. Others purchase proprietary front office systems like REMOS or Reuters which were amongst the earliest. Today many partial and complete software solutions are offered. In general, the more sophisticated and automated the front office system, the less manual processing and calculating is required.

Whatever the system, the component parts are consistent. So what are they?

Deal ticket encoding

All banks have a system for encoding new deal tickets. Encoding serves to identify the counterparty with whom the host bank has traded. There are many ways to achieve this, usually a unique number or mnemonic is used which will then display the full name and postal/SWIFT address of the counterparty. This code will often also be used to help to collate data regarding the host bank's exposure to particular counterparties in terms of amounts and also by the industrial sector for corporate clients.

Swapping instructions

Having first been entered into the dealer's front end system the deal ticket must then be passed electronically or manually to the back office for processing and settlement (ie, payment of the sold or loaned currency and/or receipt of the purchased currency or repaid loan).

In order to be able to execute such payments, the back office must know or find out the payment instructions of the counterparty. There are several different ways and stages at which a bank can add delivery instructions to a deal ticket and this has to be done in accordance with their internal policy. Some dealers will leave all the settlement instructions to be added by their back office. Some dealers will add instructions to deals with overseas counterparties but request the back office to add instructions to deals with local counterparties. Some banks endeavour to use SSIs on all or just selected counterparties. It may also be possible that different SSIs are exchanged for different types of operation, for example, a different nostro in the same currency for FX, MM and bond transactions.

Standing settlement instruction (SSI) agreements

An SSI agreement is a legally binding arrangement established between two parties. The objective of the agreement is very simple. Normally, without an SSI agreement, the two parties involved in a trade would have to either exchange delivery instructions via the dealing medium (eg, broker or Reuters) when the deal is struck if they were in different countries or exchange instructions by telephone if they were both in the same country.

When two parties sign and commence an SSI agreement, they advise each other at which nostro correspondent they will *always* take delivery of specified currencies. Therefore, on all future trades, there is no need to advise one another where they receive traded currencies as this has already been established. An SSI agreement is also known as a 'non-swapping agreement' as the two parties involved no longer have to swap instruction on all of their future trades.

Therefore, for example, if Bank A and Bank B enter into an SSI agreement, every time Bank A sells or loans Bank B some yen, there is no need to swap instructions as Bank A *already* knows that Bank B *always* takes delivery of its JPY at say, Mitsubishi-Tokyo, Tokyo.

The use of SSIs is growing each year and some central banks issue guidelines and advice on the best practice which should be used in such agreements, for example, advising the minimum notice period which should be given when one party has changed its nostro correspondent in a particular currency.

SSI agreements are popular because they reduce processing costs and reduce the risks of both error and fraud. Additionally, SSI agreements help facilitate straight-through processing of deals. The Bank of England recommends that SSIs be exchanged by SWIFT (London Code of Conduct, p.14, s. 100-105 and Schedule 2).

One possible problem with SSIs is that, since instructions are not sought on a deal-by-deal basis, a deal could be processed and payments sent on a deal which has been incorrectly recorded between two institutions. This would only be possible on deals done over the phone or via a broker between two institutions in the same centre and would normally be discovered before payments are sent, but on short date trades the problem becomes greater. Obtaining the return of funds then can become quite time-consuming and problematical for reconciliation. (BART and TRAM would obviously assist here - see Appendix 3). It devolves upon the back office to ensure that all SSI details are monitored, including:

- The original exchange.
- Updates.
- Schedules for renewals.
- Input into internal processing system.
- The format of advice, ie, fax or telephone is not sufficient on its own.

An *exception* to the use of SSIs exists in many banks *in London* in respect of *deals done today for either value today or tomorrow.* The rationale for this is that confirmations would possibly not be exchanged in time - even to get matched via TRAM - before payment is due.

Validation of data

The treasury back office is where monetary payments are made and, as such, strict procedures and internal controls are necessary to avoid the risk of unauthorised payments being made and to protect the bank and its customers generally. This is especially relevant in the case of requests for amendments to details - reports to management on details of amended details is a good control. In forward FX swaps, amendments have to be very carefully monitored, for if the first leg has already matured and the swap details are subsequently amended, the true profitability will be affected unless the points differential between the spot and forward leg is maintained.

Each bank will have its own internal controls and policies to ensure the accuracy and validity of deal data and to make sure that each new deal received in the back office from the dealing room is a genuine and bona fide transaction. The things to check are that no basic data is missing, a Reuters slip is attached when it should be, etc.

Most computer systems are designed with a series of checks and balances to ensure that the deal ticket received by the back office is valid and accurate. Some banks may also have a policy of ensuring that either a broker or counterparty confirmation is received before the payment on the trade can be released. Other banks check each Reuters dealing slip against each trade prior to executing payment. The variation on the overall theme of the need to validate before making irrevocable release of a payment will relate back to the degree of automation employed in the overall processing operation.

Straight-through processing could be a problem here, but only if the initial set-up was not originally validated. For manual or semi-automated operations, the two major hang-ups could be release against one signature when more than one required and lack of authorised signatories at time-sensitive moments (eg, last cut off for value same day payments).

There are a variety of ways to ensure the integrity of deal data. However, each bank must satisfy itself and usually its local banking regulatory authority that its system is as fraud-proof as possible.

Third party payments

There are situations where the purchaser, borrower or the 'normal' beneficiary of funds may require the paying bank to execute its payment to a beneficiary other than itself. In other words the host bank's counterparty requests that the funds actually due to it be paid to a third party. Whereas in the vast majority of instances, the counterparty requires the payment to be made directly to its own account, the paying bank is executing a third party payment and thus runs the risk of these funds being fraudulently diverted into an unauthorised account.

Every bank takes a number of measures to protect itself from this risk of loss and, indeed, some banks refuse altogether to make third party payments because of the inherent risk. One method that can be used to reduce this particular risk is for banks to insist on receiving special mandates or authorisation from their customers who require such third party payments to be made. Such authorisations from the counterparty to the paying bank would normally state specifically the currencies, the maximum amounts and the individuals employed by the organisation who are authorised to request such payments. The mandate may even specify the actual names of the only third party beneficiaries that may be entertained. Also there may be other controls in place such as the requirement to phone back a different-named individual at the company to the one who gave the original instruction or even code words may be used.

Where the special mandates do exist, it is then the responsibility of the paying bank to ensure that the customer's and bank's instructions are followed precisely. There remains, of course, the risk of collusion between members of staff employed by the bank, the customer's institution or both. However, each bank must be aware of the dangers and employ appropriate measures and practices to combat the risk of fraud.

Releasing confirmations/payments

Because of the ever-present risk of fraud inside financial institutions, all back offices should have a system whereby at least two individuals are required to release trades. This is particularly the case where the actual deal payment is being released. Some banks' systems have the functionality to require a *third* person to verify the release of a payment, particularly when there is an exceptionally large amount involved, if it is a third party payment or if payment is contingent upon some other event .

Since some correspondents will only action a maximum amount of payments before matching amounts received - so-called daylight exposure limit - it is important that priority payments are released ahead of others and that the current total of payments in progress is monitored to avoid any embarrassment with both the agent and the recipient.

Treatment of exceptions

Where discrepancies arise between the host bank's own record of the deal and the incoming broker or counterparty confirmation, these differences must be advised to the dealing room as quickly as possible. However, it is imperative that control procedures are always adhered to and that contact between the front and back office in such situations is strictly in accordance with established lines of communications. Some banks have a strict policy whereby dealing personnel are not allowed in the back office and only selected back office staff are allowed to enter the dealing room.

A good general rule of thumb is that original incoming confirmations which are unidentified or which have discrepancies should never be left with the dealer who would have struck the trade if it were genuine, but should be presented to the head of section to be referred to the appropriate dealer. However this is not a rule applicable to all banks. (BART and TRAM again are relevant to this process, see Appendix 3.)

Payments

Value dates

Every foreign exchange transaction has a value date. The value date is the precise date on which the host bank must deliver to its counterparty the currency which was sold to it under the contract. Similarly, the counterparty to the deal must deliver the currency (countervalue) amount purchased by the host bank on the same day (ie, the value date). Care is needed to ensure that deals are not inadvertently written for holidays in the host country of the currency - regular updating of the database with holidays is necessary to avoid unnecessary reprocessing. Most automated systems will usually highlight any deals dealt for an apparent holiday for one or other of the currencies involved and require 'a manual override' if it is to be ignored. (This is unlikely to continue to be a problem after the introduction of the single currency since some countries which are currently members of the Exchange Rate Mechanism (ERM) are rather dilatory in declaring their national holidays which impact upon value dates for the ECU. Some even change them subsequently, thus this override facility is required.)

It is imperative that the host bank executes payment of the sold currency on the exact date agreed in the contract. Failure to do so will result in an interest claim being lodged on the host bank by the counterparty for late receipt of its funds. Similarly, where the host bank is due to receive funds from its counterparty into a nostro (or vostro) account, it is also imperative that the funds are received on the contracted value date. Upon reconciling nostro (and vostro) accounts, failure to notice where incoming funds have been received late or outgoing payments have been effected with an earlier value date than instructed, will result in overdraft interest charges being incurred. The introduction of the euro will put some extra pressure on the back office since value same day and value tomorrow transactions will increase significantly.

Maturity dates

Whereas a foreign exchange deal has only one value date being the date on which the two currencies must be exchanged by the buyer and seller, a money market deal in effect has two value dates. The first value date is the date on which the lender of the monies must deliver the currency to the borrower. The second value date is the date on which the borrower of the monies must return the principal amount, together with all accrued interest, to the lender. This second value date in money market parlance is known officially as the *maturity date.*

Payment methods

One of the most important aspects of the deal process is the outgoing payment. The way the payment is made will depend on how well integrated the host bank's systems are as well as how automated its payment system is. With the use of the latest technology and by using SSIs, highly automated banks can achieve straight-through processed rates in the region of 80 or 90%. In other words, once the deal is struck and it passes a series of automated validity checks, a confirmation and payment order can be automatically generated and merely awaits final (human) verification before being released.

Normally, such confirmations (MT300/MT320) and payments (MT100/MT202/MT203) are sent via the SWIFT network. SWIFT, or the Society for World-wide Interbank Financial Telecommunications, was established in 1977. It is owned by a consortium of international banks and owes much of its success to the standardisation of financial messages such as confirmations, payments, statements and advices. SWIFT operates in 5,300 financial institutions in over 137 countries and continues to grow.

Each field or piece of data on a SWIFT message has an internationally recognised reference number and each field must be structured in a particular manner thereby helping to make all SWIFT messages easily understood. It is vital that the correct message form is used per transaction type as the cancelling of a SWIFT message and/or the return of funds will always have its problems - especially where 'use of funds' compensation is requested by the institution which incorrectly paid funds. (In the USA standard rules now apply to any such request regarding 'undue enrichment' covering reserve requirements and penalty charges per transaction.)

Banks which are non-SWIFT users must continue to use the postal service for sending confirmations and to use tested telexes for executing their payment orders. A tested telex is one which is authenticated by the sender to ensure the security and authenticity of the message (see later section, cash management, on page 48).

Deadlines

For the majority of the world's currencies which are traded in the foreign exchange and money markets, it is normally sufficient to give one day's notice of payment from the sending/ordering bank to the receiving/paying bank. In other words if, for example, a CHF payment order was being sent by a UK bank to a bank in Switzerland for value Monday 21/10, the payment order should be sent from the British bank to the Swiss bank by the close of business on the 18/10 to ensure that the beneficiary received good value 21/10.

Most deadlines for the payment of currencies for value the same day are before 12 midday on the value date (USD and GBP are notable exceptions) - but it is imperative that back office staff are aware of *all* deadlines by currency. A payment deadline or cut-off time is the latest time which the payment order can be received by the paying bank from the ordering bank to guarantee that good value will be applied to the beneficiary's account.

If using particular agents (Cedel/Euroclear/CHIPS or CHAPS) they have their own requirements, for example, the rules for CHAPS state that a payment received by a bank, which it is unable to apply, must be returned by it to the remitter by 12 noon on the following business day in order to avoid incurring cost. It is essential the back office staff are aware of such matters, especially when changes of staff/holidays occur.

The deadline becomes very important over Easter and especially at Christmas and New Year when different countries have different holidays and cut-off times are often varied to allow for these and the fact that banks work on skeleton staff. For the euro TARGET currently will only close on Christmas day and New Year's day.

Receipt of payment orders after the deadline will (usually) result in the payment being executed on the next available business day. In such cases, the ordering bank will receive an interest claim from the beneficiary bank for the late receipt of funds and this will result in a monetary loss to the ordering bank.

The back office must therefore always be aware of the respective cut-off times for the various traded currencies. Additionally, some currencies such as the Saudi Arabian riyal (SAR) require a minimum of two days' notice and some individual banks may impose their deadlines which may differ from the generally accepted deadlines in that country.

Netting

Although the overall concept of netting is valid - ie, avoiding gross settlement of each individual trade and thereby reducing the volume of trades to be settled and the concomitant settlement risk - it adds a further onus on the back office. Netting is also a tool for reducing risk.

The choice of netting can vary considerably: *bilateral* - two banks, one centre, one currency; two banks, one centre, more than one currency; two banks, one currency, more than one centre and two banks, all centres more than one currency and *multilateral* - clearing house (Echo or Multinet, now CLS bank).

In essence, only an automated netting system can work without placing undue stress on the human factor. Payment netting involving two counterparties results in the offsetting of funds payable to and receivable from each other to arrive at a situation where only one net payment is made (per currency).

Close-out netting
Back office should only become involved in this once a decision has been made elsewhere. For close-out netting only comes into force when a counterparty goes bankrupt and/or defaults. Reference to the back office would mainly involve the provision of all outstanding contracts and mark-to-market prices for those positions, see page 91 for a detailed example.

Clearing and payment systems

Clearing
In the majority of cases, when a bank is settling a foreign currency transaction, it will use the services provided by its nostro account bank to execute the payment in favour of the beneficiary. However, where the payment is to be made to the beneficiary in *local currency*, normally, the local payment clearing system is used. Individual clearing systems may be owned and operated by a consortium of local banks or they may be operated and controlled by a country's central bank.

In essence, the function of the clearing house from where the clearing system operates is to allow each member bank to settle daily all monies payable to and receivable from all other members of that payment clearing system. Rather than physically make hundreds of payments to each other every day, the net position (funds receivable against funds payable) is calculated for each bank with each other member and each bank would then either receive or make only one payment to every other member of the clearing.

In the USA, the USD clearing system is known as CHIPS or Clearing House Interbank Payment System. In the UK, the clearing system is known as

CHAPS or Clearing House Automated Payments System. Each country has its own local payment clearing system which is usually located in the main financial centre or the capital city. All clearing systems have their own rules and regulations devised to ensure fair and efficient running. For example, the rules for CHAPS state that a payment received by a bank, which it is unable to apply, must be returned by it to the remitter by *12 noon on the following business day* in order to avoid incurring cost. CHAPS is one of three clearing companies that forms the Association for Payment Clearing Services (APACS). CHAPS only accounts for 0.3% of APACS' volumes but 92% of value. BACS (Banks Automated Clearing Services) and Cheque & Credit Clearing Company are the other two.

Banks which are not members of their local payments clearing system must employ the services of a bank which is a member in order to execute their own payments in the local currency.

Vostro accounts

Treasury business is undertaken in the majority of the world's major currencies and the use of nostro accounts for the settlement of cross-border payments will be described in Chapter 4. In the same way that a host bank needs to own and operate a nostro account held overseas to settle its foreign currency transactions, banks overseas have an identical need to effect cross-border payments in the host bank's local currency. Therefore, if, for example, a bank in the USA opened an account with a bank located in the UK and that account was denominated in pounds sterling, that account in the UK is known as a vostro account. Therefore, a vostro account is essentially an account owned by an overseas bank and maintained in the host bank's local currency.

However, whereas a bank's nostro account is normally monitored and funded by that bank's nostro reconciliation's department, the responsibility for monitoring and funding vostro accounts is normally held by the host bank's accounts department.

In the same way that a bank may own more than one nostro account, usually for operational purposes - one for FX settlements, one for MM - banks overseas may also operate more than one vostro account in the same currency. Responsibility for ensuring adequate funding on vostro accounts lies with the holder/owner of the vostro account as overdraft interest charges can be incurred on them in the same manner as with nostro accounts.

Herstatt risk

Because of the need of each bank to execute its foreign currency payment orders in advance of known cut-off times, this normally involves the despatching of its payment orders to its nostro correspondent bank at least one day prior to the required value date.

Herstatt risk refers to each situation where a bank in one country effecting a payment in favour of a bank in another country is faced with the possibility that, overnight, the counterparty to the transaction to whom the funds were paid, is unable to settle its side of the (eg, foreign exchange) transaction owing to bankruptcy being declared by that counterparty.

Herstatt Bank was a medium-sized West German bank which, in 1974, became insolvent and was therefore unable to meet its payment commitments to its international counterparty banks who had already paid funds to it without the knowledge of Herstatt Bank's impending bankruptcy.

All banks run this risk and attempt to reduce the potential for loss in this way. By setting maximum dealing limits with each of their counterparties with whom they trade, a bank can reduce its exposure to individual banks. Many banks also join payment netting schemes which mitigate the potential for loss owing to Herstatt risk as the sums due from and payable to each counterparty are netted out, thereby reducing their actual exposure to that bank. Additionally, by delaying the transmission of their payment order from a spot (or earlier) date to just one day prior to the value date, this further reduces the possibility of monetary loss owing to Herstatt risk.

Non-standard settlement instruments

Certificates of deposit (CDs)

A regular, but slightly more complicated, function of the back office is the settlement of secondary CDs or other negotiable instruments (commercial paper, bankers' acceptances and Treasury bills). However, once the formula is mastered, there is merely a mechanical calculation to be done.

According to the currency, there may be a secondary function required - that of arranging delivery. To avoid the need to have the physical transfer of bearer instruments arranged - some robberies have occurred in the past - in London for USD securities, First Chicago Clearing Centre (FCCC) operates a depository, and for GBP securities, the Bank of England operates the Central Moneymarkets Office (CMO) for bills and CDs and the Central Gilts Office (CGO) for gilts and £ debentures. The settlement procedure is 90% DVP (delivery versus payment), ie, delivery or advice to the depository to move the security to the new owner will release the actual cash.

Discounted instruments

These are commercial paper, Treasury bills and bankers' acceptances, where the face value (FV) is discounted so that the amount paid away by the lender is always less than face value. Back office's role, under today's degree of mechanisation, would be limited to random checks that the correct formula has been applied. Thus, for UK bills - mostly issued for three or six months in face values of GBP 1,000,000 - if we take a 90-day issue at 10%, using the appropriate formula the proceeds will be:

$$\text{Proceeds} = FV - \left[FV \left(\frac{T \times DR}{B \times 100} \right) \right]$$

$$= 1{,}000{,}000 - \left[1{,}000{,}000 \left(\frac{90 \times 10}{36500} \right) \right]$$

$$= 1{,}000{,}000 - 24{,}657.53 = 975{,}342.47$$

where:
FV	=	Face value
T	=	Time
DR	=	Discount rate
B	=	Base (360 or 365 days)

Non-deliverable forwards

In pure foreign exchange terms non-deliverable forwards (NDFs) have allowed speculation in a currency's future value which could not otherwise be achieved since there were restrictions on what transactions qualified for forward cover (ie, trade only) or the market was illiquid. The currencies tend to be the more exotic currencies, for example, Mexican peso, Malaysian ringgit, Indonesian rupiah, etc.

After a forward price has been agreed between the two counterparties, either the market user can go back before maturity and settle just the difference between original contract rate and rate now current for that date.

This leaves you open to being 'read', or you wait until the original forward date and then offset at difference spot/original contract rate.

Example - buyer of NDF in $ amount

If the fixing rate is greater than the outright price at maturity, the purchaser of the NDF will receive from the seller the difference between the fixing rate and the outright rate in cash terms. This amount can be calculated as follows:

$$\frac{(F - O) \times N}{F}$$

where F = fixing rate, O = outright price and N = notional amount. Obviously, if the fixing rate is less than the outright price at maturity, the opposite will apply.

Sale example

Notional amount	USD 10,000,000.00
Maturity	90 days
Spot	2.0000 FX/USD
90-day NDF	0.0100
Outright	2.0100 FX/USD
Fixing rate	2.0200 FX/USD

At maturity the purchase of the NDF will receive from the seller:

$$\frac{(2.0200 - 2.0100 \times USD\ 10,000,000.00)}{2.0200}$$

$$\frac{0.0100 \times 10,000,000.00}{2.0200}$$

$$USD\ 49,504.95$$

In investment terms NDFs provide the opportunity to hedge cash flows from investments in more exotic currencies. This is becoming more important as investors look for higher returns than those available in current stable interest rate environments of Western Europe/USA/Japan and ahead of the single currency.

An investor wanting to benefit from the type of enhanced yield available in the emerging markets would have to do the following:

- Purchase the spot currency and sell dollars.
- Invest in a local risk-free asset (ie, a government bond).
- Fund the dollars at Libor.
- Receive the capital plus interest at maturity.
- Sell the currency on the spot market and purchase dollars.

Using an NDF the investor can hedge the FX risk inherent in the investment. In doing this he can take advantage of much greater yields; for example, the implied NDF yield on the six-month New Taiwanese dollar (NTD) is 6.5% while, on the Korean won, it is 13.5%.

The back office role in this context is that of correct encoding, input and eventual settlement. An understanding of the overall concept of NDFs, however, will always assist efficiency.

Bonds

Compared to simple money market settlements, the procedures required for bonds are more demanding. However, provided the bond being purchased/sold has been dealt in previously, your computer program will already have full details. If not then you will be required to enter all standing data. This is available on all bonds from either a Bloomberg screen or Euroclear. The most significant fact is that bonds are normally settled via Euroclear or Cedel and value is *three days ahead* (it used to be eight days). In the future it is planned to achieve same day settlement when required. Messages therefore currently need to be sent in good time.

Day conventions can be particularly important here, but the office should have a copy of these should there be any doubt (see Appendix 12). Similarly, the cross-referencing to other instruments being used as a hedge against the bond will often be required.

Most confirmations are entered into ISMA's (International Securities and Markets Association) TRAX system - the equivalent of TRAM for FX and MM. A major requirement is that every trade must be matched within half an hour of the time it was traded, otherwise there will be a fine, escalating by time. Also every bond transaction has to be reported to the supervisory body, the Securities and Futures Authority (SFA).

If the accounting function is part of your particular back office/support department, then accounts for the actual consideration (total price paid), dividends, redemptions and sinking fund will be required.

Derivative settlements

The use - or rather misuse - of derivatives has led to comments like the following: 'A derivative is like a razor. You can use it shave yourself and make yourself attractive for your girlfriend. You can slit her throat with it. Or you can use it to commit suicide.' 'Derivatives have been likened to aspirin; taken for a headache, they will make the pain go away. If you take the whole bottle at once you may kill yourself.' (Financial Times, 4 March 1995.)

It has also led to losses such as these:

- Metallgesellchaft - US$1.5/2 billion.
- Procter & Gamble - £69 million.
- Atlantic Richfield - US$22 million.
- Barings Bank - £820 million.
- Orange County in California - US$3 to 5 billion.
- Hammersmith and Fulham - £80 million.

Whilst these are examples of front office and/or management misuse, back office equally has to be most vigilant in its role/responsibility for monitoring and settling such transactions.

The past 10 to 15 years have seen an explosive growth in the volumes of derivative products traded under the relatively new science known as financial engineering. There is a wide variety of such products available for both speculative and hedging purposes. In essence, a derivative product is a financial instrument which was *derived* from another core financial product based on an interest or an exchange rate (see Table 3.1). Derivatives were developed to help financial institutions and investment professionals to better manage their investment strategies. These instruments have names such as caps, collars, floors, options, swaps, interest rate swaps, swaptions and currency options, to name but a few. Some, such as futures are highly standardised in terms of amounts and maturities whilst others, such as options, can be tailor made to suit individual clients. Additionally, some can only be traded in highly regulated markets known as exchanges, while others can be traded in the Over The Counter (OTC) Market.

Table 3.1 The historical impetus to the growth of derivatives.

	Developments	Innovations
1982		Philadelphia Exchange, currency options, currency swaps
	Reagan recovery	
1981		
	Federal Reserve to target money and not interest rates	
1980		LIFFE, Big Bang hits London
1979		NY Futures Exchange
1978	European Monetary System	
1977	Another attempt at exchange rate stability: Jamaica accords	NY Mercantile Exchange energy futures
1976		
	Recession	.
1975		
	Volatile interest rates	Interest rate futures
1974		
	Commodity price swings	Growing interest in commodity futures
1973		
	Managed floating rates	
1972		
	The end of gold convertibility	
1971		
	The collapse of Bretton Woods	Chicago Mercantile Exchange, currency futures

Derivatives can be used either by companies which are risk-averse in order to lock into an exchange or interest thereby reducing their exposure to interest and/or exchange rate fluctuations, or they can be used by investors to speculate on commodities and even on the stock market.

Future rate agreements (FRAs) were one of the first to emerge and were the replacement for forward/forward interest rates. The latter were very difficult to arrange and only a few banks would quote them despite the need for treasurers to be able to hedge interest rate risk they knew they would have in the future. Together with the effect on the balance sheet and the filling-up of limits, the need led to the introduction of FRAs. As far as back office is concerned, the participation comes at both the arrangement of the FRA - confirming dates, rate, amount, etc, - and at maturity (the actual start date of the FRA) when the settlement amount has to be agreed (on FRABBA terms) and paid.

Let's look at an example, using the formula in Appendix 11.

Example
If a USD 20,000,000 FRA was sold at 7.10 for a 6/12 period and LIBOR is eventually fixed at 6.57, what amount of interest is payable/receivable?

$$\frac{(7.10 - 6.57) \times 183 \times 20,000,000}{(183 \times 7.10) + (360 \times 100)} = \frac{1,939,800,000}{37,299.30} = 52,006.33792$$

Currency options
Back office participation only occurs inasmuch as agreeing the terms of such options and ensuring the premium is paid/received and the resultant processing is done. For, at maturity, either the Option expires worthless - nothing to be done by back office - or the option is exercised. Then exercise means that a spot transaction will be written between the bank and the holder which will be settled in the normal way for that type of transaction. What, in the context of the mutual co-operation between front and back office, is important is that certain attributes of options contracts are understood, ie, if a customer tries to exercise a European option other than at maturity, it is not allowed. In contrast, an American style option can be exercised at any time during the life of that deal.

Futures
These exist both as currency and interest rate futures, but it is really only

the interest rate futures that have had any impact in Europe. This results from the fact that currency futures do not offer a significant advantage - in terms of the use of capital - over forward foreign exchange. Interest rate futures do offer much more versatility against straight cash - no principal being exchanged, good leverage acquired via cost of *initial margin* compared to size of contract owned - and thus are more popular. (See Figure 3.1 for an example of growth.)

Because financial futures can only be traded on regulated exchanges, there is no counterparty risk of default. However, because of this, the underlying instrument is 'marked to market' (or revalued) on a daily basis which may necessitate the counterparty making a *variation margin* payment to the exchange to reflect the notionally reduced value of the underlying asset being traded - this is where the back office support is required. (There is a list of some of the contracts on LIFFE in Appendix 14.)

The back office has several duties in conjunction with these interest rate futures:

- Keeping a track of dealers' positions.
- Reconciling dealers' positions to statements received from agents (independent revaluation from Reuters pages for 'settlement' price).
- Managing the margin account.

Let's look at an example - Table 3.2.

The points that are relevant to the back office are the checking that: outstandings agree to dealer's records, any reference is correctly stated and any additional margin is paid if the account falls below the minimum.

Late 1998 provided another warning on the dangers of the lack of management controls on derivatives. It might have led to something approaching local systemic failure since the situation could bring down a number of other participants in LIFFE.

The case in question concerned Griffin Trading Company, an American-owned company, where - as a result of the unauthorised trading of one dealer - losses of £6.2 million were incurred. The position taken by the trader - 9,000 DEM government bond futures - exceeded his trading limit by a factor of 10. Whereas LIFFE, the SFA and the German and American authorities led the investigation, something went wrong internally at the company itself and at the company processing its orders, both of whom should have

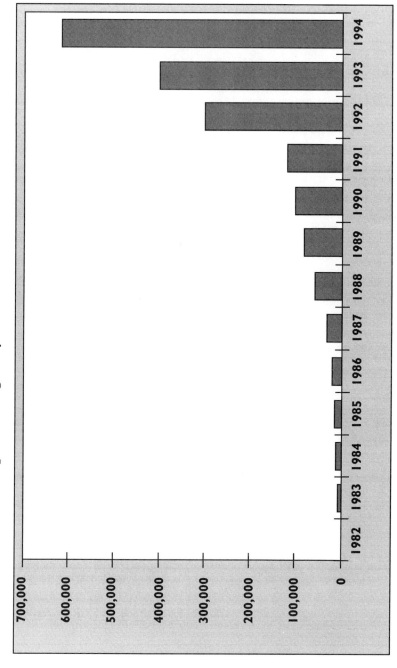

Figure 3.1 LIFFE futures and options average daily volume.

Table 3.2 A margining example.

Del month	Trade date	Price		Lots	Reference	Market price	Margin value
Ten-year treasury bond							
Mar99	20.12.96	92.430	B	2	INTF105	92.710	4702.84CR
Mar99	06.01.97	92.230	B	65	@INT SSP1	92.710	259793.95CR
Mar99	08.01.97	92.335	B	14	INTF102	92.710	43910.86CR
Mar99	17.01.97	92.540	B	15	INT F101	92.710	21515.55CR
Mar99	17.02.97	92.725	B	4	*	92.710	510.28DR
Mar99	13.01.97	92.440	S	20	INT SSP1	92.710	45368.20DR
Mar99	15.01.97	92.395	S	9	INT F101	92.710	23772.51DR
Mar99	15.01.97	92.405	S	7	INT F101	92.710	17910.41DR
Mar99	21.01.97	92.580	S	11	INT F105	92.710	12086.25DR
Mar99	30.01.97	92.425	S	12	*	92.710	28714.80DR
Mar99	03.02.97	92.520	S	16	*	92.710	25628.00DR
Mar99	03.02.97	92.585	S	8	*	92.710	8453.76DR
Mar99	04.02.97	92.625	S	30	*	92.710	21594.00DR
Mar99	04.02.97	92.635	S	1	*	92.710	635.35DR
Mar99	05.02.97	92.615	S	8	*	92.710	5083.12DR
Mar99	06.02.97	92.635	S	25	*	92.710	20103.50DR
Mar99	07.02.97	92.625	S	8	*	92.710	5083.12DR
Mar99	10.02.97	92.625	S	37	INTIR02	92.710	26632.60DR
Mar99 Futures	Total	100	B	192S			**88347.26CR**
Futures	Total	100	B	192S			**88347.26CR**
Total							**88347.26CR**

realised that the positions were well outside of the authority to trade. Since this company dealt on behalf of others, two trading companies and up to 100 individuals could lose substantial amounts as a result of this incident. Assuming the deal(s) had been written up, then some responsibility in back office would have been relevant to bring this matter to the attention of the trader and management (echoes of Barings and Nick Leeson's trading).

Interest rate swaps

These were 'invented' to help treasurers manage their borrowings by allowing them to make a judgement against the future direction and relationship of short to long interest rates. Thus, if they only had access to short-dated six month funds, but felt it would be better to borrow long dated funds, which they thought were about to rise then they would 'pay' in (say) the five year fixed and swap it for their six month funds. The opposite could also occur (see Figure 3.2, for example).

Back office involvement again would only be to agree rates between counterparties - and any intermediaries - and to communicate and agree with the counterparty the rollover rate each six months against the London inter bank offered rate (Libor) and exchange any difference (interest only). A variation which involves more care is a currency interest rate swap (CIRS) where the currencies for the fixed and floating currencies are not the same. In this case, an exchange of currencies may occur at the start date of the swap or at start and maturity - *there will always be an exchange at maturity*. Back office staff need to be vigilant here as one CIRS may differ from another, also the exchange rate must be the same at the start and at maturity.

What will be vital is that any documentation called for in conjunction with the swap is received. Normally this will be ISDA since that is now the benchmark. However, some will be individually drawn up and some could be BBAIRS.

If an institution is involved in a lot of 'financial engineering' where a bond, an IRS and some futures deals are all linked, then it will fall to the back office to ensure that the correct cross-referencing is effected - or at least that some entries have been made by front office indicating whether there are any links so that correct positions show in the position reports, management reports and P&L reports.

Repurchase agreements (repos)

Apart from the USA, repurchase agreements were late to emerge elsewhere, but they now exist anywhere there is a developed bond market.

Figure 3.2 A basic swap transaction.

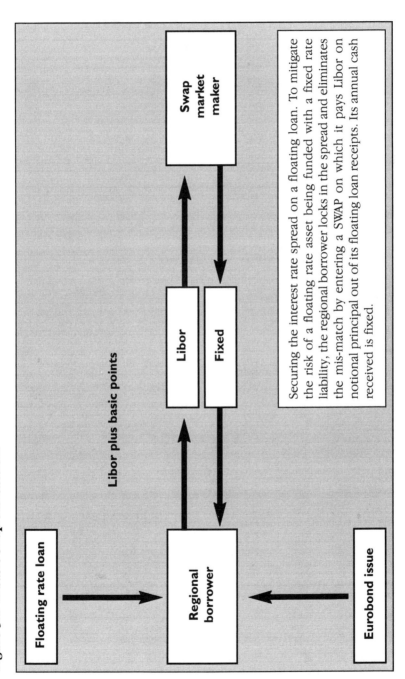

Floating rate loan

Libor plus basic points

Swap market maker

Libor

Fixed

Regional borrower

Eurobond issue

Securing the interest rate spread on a floating loan. To mitigate the risk of a floating rate asset being funded with a fixed rate liability, the regional borrower locks in the spread and eliminates the mis-match by entering a SWAP on which it pays Libor on notional principal out of its floating loan receipts. Its annual cash received is fixed.

Their use is to a holder to earn some interest on their investment or to a borrower to use them to obtain cheap short-date funding. The mechanics are that repos are arranged for very short periods where the owner (holder) 'lends' the bond for which the temporary borrower pays an interest rate which is used to calculate the difference between the price on the bond when sold and the rate on it when it is returned to the original owner.

The difficulty for back office emanates from the different types of repo operation - sell/buy-back; classic repo or securities lending - and the various ancillary duties - arrangements for delivery, margin calls and payment peculiarities. This will necessitate at least a basic understanding of the different types and their 'jargon'. Examples of each type, with variations are included in Appendix 6. However, the essential points to be grasped as a responsibility of back office are as follows:

- The movement of the bond being used as collateral.
- The 'margin' receipt/payment during the life of repo.
- The settlement will normally be via Cedel or Euroclear (see Appendix 4).

CHAPTER 4

POST-SETTLEMENT DUTIES

Confirmations

The duty of confirmations is, of course, not solely post-settlement as automation has intervened via TRAM/TRAX as have standard settlement instructions (SSIs). SWIFT users normally exchange confirmations using MT300 or MT320 messages. Highly automated banks can use these standardised messages to facilitate automatic matching of incoming confirmations. Similarly, many FX/MM brokers in Europe can also send their confirmations electronically using TRAM, banks' automated confirmation reception terminal (BART) and automated confirmation system (ACS) and this also facilitates automatic matching by the recipients of their confirmations (see Appendix 3 for full details).

The system effectively short-cuts the delivery of paper-based confirmations which would need separate generation and physical delivery to the counterparty by providing automatic electronic messages from the broker to the bank as the details are entered at the broker's office. The speed of transmission is especially useful for short-date transactions where payments have to be made almost immediately after the deal has been completed - although see Chapter 3 concerning London banks' practice on short dates. All of these can be used together with your own in-house computer or paper-based systems and the advantages are as follows:

• Speed of reconciliation.
• Reduction in boring procedures (which often result in mistakes).

- Early notice of problems.
- Easier production of management reports.

(For better reconciliation of corporate transactions two other systems exist for corporates only - FXMatch from Citibank and Concord from CityNetwork.)

Whatever the system in force for receiving/sending confirmations, in the event of non-receipt of confirmations, each institution should have an established escalation procedure to follow up missing confirmations and reports should be despatched to management.

Failure by a counterparty to send confirmation could be the first signal of impending financial failure of that counterparty in that they will not confirm transactions on which they might either lose money or be unable to settle through adverse cash flow, fraud, inefficiency, etc. Although they are no substitute for the actual counter party confirmation, a Reuters log or interim brokerage note can act as substantiating evidence for both the existence and correctness of a trade (as can taped telephone calls).

A 1999 survey by Benchmarking Technologies International (BTI) in New York emphasised the importance of the back office role in this context. The survey was of 162 US based corporate and investment clients of 16 major global banks (ranked by Euromoney as amongst the 20 top FX dealers in the world). The two areas most regularly mentioned under 'areas of concern' were 'transparency of pricing' and 'timely, accurate confirmations'. The latter was termed as 'a key service dimension' and the survey found that banks which could not provide confirmation of late trades on trade date were avoided as counterparts. Although ranking first (out of seven areas of performance surveyed) after pricing, quality of service was a close second. Furthermore, respondents were prepared to accept minor pricing differentials provided their risk was managed properly and they received efficient service on confirmations, settlements, inquiries/investigations and ease of doing business.

Cash management

Unless and until you have the answers to the following questions, an efficient management of cash resources/deficits will not be possible.

- When do we know what has happened?

- When do we have to send instructions by?
- What type of instructions have to be sent?
- What are the interest rates on the account?
- What are the market rates?

For even from one nostro holder to another in the same currency the terms for credit/debit balances can vary. The attention to detail in moving money around to maximise income or minimise cost can thus be one means of further enhancing the front office/back office relationship.

The major 'players' in the Treasury market conclude high volumes of transactions - 5,000 - plus deals per day per bank are now fairly commonplace in the major financial centres such as London and New York. Where a bank's dealers may not have left a perfectly 'square' overnight position, surplus funds held on nostro accounts together with other 'uncleared' items relating to trade finance instruments which have not yet debited from the nostro accounts, means that funds remain available for investment on overnight deposit.

As banks continue to seek to maximise their revenues, the management and investment of temporarily available cash has grown to be an important function in many back office operations and contributes significantly to the banks' overall profitability. However, in a particularly active institution, many different areas of operation - FX, MM, bonds, futures and swaps - may all generate cash flow, thus a separate section may handle the net position.

By closely monitoring the activity and balances on their accounts, many banks are able to shrewdly invest (usually) overnight these temporarily available surplus funds in the currency's local market thereby earning interest on their deposits. Often successful management of funds depends on fostering good personal relationships with the person(s) responsible for your nostro.

This was especially relevant in the 1970s when both Germany and Switzerland were trying to avoid major revaluations of their currencies. To effect this, they introduced 'negative' interest rates and imposed a maximum size of balance that any bank could hold on its account (based on average balances over a preceding period). On balances above that figure, large penalties would be imposed. Japan also later imposed something similar by not accepting payments into an account unless it had matching amounts to be paid out.

Even in normal times, the back office staff should keep a close watch on incoming statements from correspondent banks to monitor when overdraft interest rates change. This information should be passed on to not only all the other members of the office but also to dealers so that they are aware of the possible consequences of overdrawing their account.

Naturally, it is essential that all the nostro accounts have first been adequately funded as invariably credit interest rates are lower than overdraft interest rates and an account left overdrawn while 'surplus' funds have been invested will result in a net loss to the bank as the deposit interest earned may not cover any overdraft charges incurred.

Reconciliations

Part of the function of the back office, is to reconcile the various accounts used when transacting the treasury business. The reconciliations department is responsible for ensuring that any outstanding amounts are promptly investigated and resolved either by itself or perhaps by its treasury investigations department.

Nostro reconciliations

A nostro account is an account owned by the host bank and maintained with a bank (usually) overseas. The account is denominated in the local currency of the foreign bank and is used by the host bank for settling its treasury business in that particular currency. Therefore, for example, a bank in London which undertakes treasury activity in US dollars will need to open a US dollar account with a bank located in the USA. Each time the host bank in the UK needs to make a payment in USD, it will send an authenticated instruction to its nostro correspondent bank in the USA requesting it to execute the payment. Also, where the bank in London is due to *receive* a USD payment, it will instruct its counterparty to effect the payment to its nostro account held in the USA.

In order for the nostro bank to be sure that the telegraphic/SWIFT payment instruction which it received from the UK bank is genuine and was sent by the true owner of the account, every payment order has to be authenticated. The process of authentication requires the two banks concerned to exchange 'test keys'. Test keys are secret codes which are known and understood only by the two banks concerned. The construction of the test keys usually involve (in coded format) the amount of the payment order and the date on which it was transmitted by the host bank to its nostro correspondent bank.

Given the fact that anyone who has access to these confidential test keys will have access to the funds in the bank's nostro accounts, it is essential that each bank's test keys are held in a highly secure area usually within its telecommunications department. Also it is vital that the person(s) empowered to effect nostro reconciliation is not also someone who originates transactions (ie, from front office) or anyone who makes/releases payments. This is obviously necessary to avoid any internal 'wrong-doings' or collusion. (See also page 100.)

Essentially there are six factors, as follow, which may be the cause of an unexpected nostro balance, where:

- A bank expects to receive funds and does not.
- A bank expects to receive funds and receives the wrong amount.
- A bank receives funds and did not expect to receive them.
- A bank expects to pay funds and does not.
- A bank expects to pay funds and pays the wrong amount.
- A bank pays funds and did not expect to pay them.

Nostro statements

In the same way that we all receive a statement from our bank where our current account is held, the host bank will receive a statement for each nostro account it holds in order that it can check and verify the accuracy of each entry on its account. However, where individuals would normally receive a statement from their bank only monthly, because of the size of the entries and the sheer volume of items, statements on nostro accounts are usually produced and sent by the nostro correspondent on a daily basis (or whenever there is activity/movement over the account).

Statement despatch

If the nostro bank is not a SWIFT user, it will normally send statements to the account holder by mail. However, this method has certain disadvantages as any delay in reconciling the statement can lead to errors taking longer to come to light and can therefore lead to monetary losses being incurred. Generally, therefore, banks are normally only prepared to accept posted statements where the activity is low to moderate. It is fairly common for such statements to be first sent via fax before the mailed copy is despatched. This enables the account holder to reconcile its account more promptly, thereby allowing earlier notification of possible errors.

The majority of nostro account statements are now sent via the SWIFT network, usually by way of an MT950 or sometimes an MT940. Apart from the high speed at which they can be sent, there is another huge advantage which SWIFT statements have over their mailed versions. Because of the very structured and standardised manner in which SWIFT statements are formatted, they can be electronically downloaded into the host bank's accounting computer system upon receipt. This facilitates the automatic reconciliation (by computer) of many of the entries on the account against the host bank's own internal records of its transactions and therefore reduces considerably the amount of manual (visual) reconciling that needs to be done.

Book-keeping

Many banks operate what is known as a double-entry book-keeping system. This means simply that each time the host bank makes or is due to receive a payment, a corresponding entry is passed on an internal general ledger account which is associated with the relevant nostro account. Therefore, when funds are expected on a nostro account a general ledger *debit* is passed internally over the related account. Upon receipt of the funds by the nostro correspondent, the relevant *credit* will appear on the account. On reconciling the account, the statement credit is reconciled against the ledger debit.

Conversely, upon issuing instructions to the nostro correspondent to execute a payment, the host bank will generate a credit on the related general ledger. Once the nostro bank has made the payment it will debit the host bank's nostro account and this entry will appear on the nostro statement. Once again, upon reconciling the account, the general ledger credit should be matched off against the debit which appears on the statement.

The reconciliations department must ensure that, for each ledger debit and ledger credit that is passed, the nostro account statement should reflect the respective credit and debit in terms of *amount, reference* (or *counterparty*) and *value date*. Failure to correctly reconcile (mismatching) items can lead to an array of problems such as being unaware of valid payments not executed, claiming non-receipt of funds from the wrong counterparty and unwittingly incurring overdraft interest on the nostro account.

As such, absolute vigilance and attention to detail is essential when reconciling the bank's nostro accounts.

Nostro investigations

An outstanding amount on a general ledger or nostro account is often the first indication that a problem exists with a particular transaction. In very broad terms, the following examples serve only to illustrate the types of problems which may arise and the reasons why.

• Outstanding ledger debit - may indicate that funds receivable have not been received.

• Outstanding ledger credit - could mean the host bank has failed to execute a payment.

• Outstanding statement credit - may indicate that the host bank has failed to record a deal.

• Outstanding statement debit - could indicate a deal cancelled (in error) or entry passed by nostro bank in error.

The above examples are not definitive but merely show some potential reasons for unreconciled items. Each investigation needs to be handled individually and usually requires reference to the original source document such as the broker's note or Reuters dealing slip.

CHAPTER 5

▌▌▌

ANCILLARY RESPONSIBILITIES

Limits/exposure

One of the functions of the deal capture process is to record and update the host bank's records for limit purposes. Each host bank will normally set a maximum trading *limit* with each counterparty with whom it trades. Individual limits are set in order to monitor the host bank's *exposure* to each of its dealing counterparties. The host bank's exposure to a particular counterparty reflects the maximum monetary amount which the host bank may lose in the event of that counterparty defaulting on its outstanding deals (owing to insolvency or bankruptcy). It is therefore important that a bank can ascertain on a real-time basis, at any stage during the business day, exactly what its current limit and exposure may be with any one of its trading partners. These limits are usually set based on the counterparty's financial size and strength.

Thus, although the prime responsibility for checking a dealing limit remains with front office, incorrect input - whether by name of bank, geographical location or status - will invalidate many vital reports which are used by management to monitor risk.

Similarly, there is a need for back office staff to understand the implications of incorrect input and trained to look out for potential errors, eg, Deutsche Bank - if a full branch the limit is fully available, if it is not a full branch, then a subsidiary limit is required and, if the branch is outside the Organisation for Economic Co-operative Development (OECD), then the risk itself and the risk weighting in respect of VaR is very different.

Dealer's position

Whilst on the face of it, the dealer's position is his responsibility, the back office is instrumental in ensuring that front to back office records agree. Thus it will often be a set procedure that dealers and back office have to agree open positions up to three times per day - at opening, at noon and at close of day. Again, depending of the *modus operandi* of each individual bank and the sophistication of its computer systems, it may be that at this stage of the deal capture process, the dealer's position is updated either automatically or manually.

The dealer's open (currency) position reflects whether that dealer is long (overbought the currency) or short (oversold the currency) or square (neither long nor short, ie, total purchases match total sales of the currency). An unwanted long or short open position which is held overnight (or overlong intraday) can lead to a monetary loss to the dealer especially in a volatile market where the exchange rate of the currency position being held moves against the dealer in the market.

Profit and loss accounting

This step flows from the previous one in that the accurate recording of positions is the first step in assessing profitability. Once the net open position and average rate has been calculated by the system a 'reference' rate can be entered. When compared to a reference rate, the system may be able to determine the profit (or loss) made on each new deal. In today's market, most dealers are paid bonuses based solely on their dealing performance and their profitability to their bank employers. Therefore, dealers will always be very interested in their P&L figures and these *may* be available to the dealer on demand during the day. P&L statements are also usually produced at the close of business each day/week/month/quarter and at the financial year end.

Depending on the internal policy and control procedures of each bank, the back office may be called upon to verify the accuracy of the dealer's daily P&L figures. This role may also extend to an involvement in full responsibility for revaluation/ marking-to-market of your institution's total portfolio.

Here, the main essential is that all rates used are obtained from independent sources, ie, front office (dealers) are not allowed:

- To supply rates themselves.
- To suggest sources you should use to obtain valuations.
- To receive originals of rates input which in any way could lead to some 'amendment' by them

Back office staff need to present a strong front in refusing to be induced to depart from the correct procedures. Any undue pressure from front office should be reported to a senior manager (note the importance of separate reporting lines again).

Brokerage

Whereas many banks do conclude Treasury business directly with each other via the telephone, telex or Reuters, the majority also use brokers as intermediaries. The broker, having successfully brokered a deal between two banks, will charge a commission for bringing the two parties together. The broker will then formally confirm the details of the transaction to both parties by mail, or increasingly now, by electronic means. Both parties are required to check the details stated in the broker's confirmation to ensure the accuracy of the deal and the amount of brokerage charged.

The actual commission or brokerage charged to the banks by the broker will vary according to the currency, the amount, the term (spot or forward) of the deal and whatever commission rates have been agreed individually with each bank. Brokers' switches must be clearly distinguished from normal deals via a broker to provide justification for the transaction, an explanation of any different rate of brokerage and form a basis for management reports.

It is normally a function of the back office to not only conduct a daily check of brokers' confirmations received (and to investigate and resolve all investigations thereon) but also to receive and check, prior to payment, the brokers' monthly invoices/statements (London Code of Conduct, p.16, s.114 onwards).

Money laundering

Previously, strong competition amongst banks for customer deposits had led to a situation where it was relatively easy for international and local drug dealers to launder the proceeds from drug-trafficking through the banking/financial industry. Many governments have since passed tough legislation requiring the financial industry to advise the police authorities even if they only suspect that an organisation is being used to 'legitimise' any illegally-obtained monies.

All banks have a legal obligation to report any suspicions they may have and there are penalties for companies who flout the law in this respect. Each bank will have its own method of alerting its staff. In the UK the Bank of England has issued specific instructions - with a video - and members of staff are required to sign to the effect that they have seen and read the relevant material. Furthermore, the Bank of England, at its bi-annual meeting with each bank operating in London, will request confirmation that all existing - and especially - new staff have been required to sign accordingly.

Once any suspicion has been notified to the MLRO (money laundering reporting officer), who may or may not refer it on, back office responsibility is fulfilled. The transaction should proceed as normal, since the funds will more likely than not turn up on time, thus it will be up to the police whether they make any attempt to void the transaction or arrest the people behind the transaction. In addition to establishing the procedures for monitoring such sources of funds and educating the staff what to look out for, it is imperative that the MLRO has sufficient status and power to access records when any suspicions are aroused.

With the creation of the euro, further fears are being expressed about the increased scope for money laundering. This fear has been voiced to the OECD by a special task force which is drawn from 26 governments as well as the European Commission and the Gulf Co-operation Council. The fear is that it will become easier for the criminally-inclined to disguise the origin of funds when a single currency is applied to a series of nations. A euro becomes characterless/unidentifiable when it could emanate from any country - France, Germany, the Netherlands, Luxembourg, Ireland, etc, thereby making the tracking that much more difficult. (Funds from Russia - estimated at some $60 billion - were of especial concern.) It will become much easier to change the identity of illegally obtained money so that it appears to have originated from a legitimate source - the point of entry for a euro becomes multiple and quickly becomes anonymous; the exit point can be equally disguised.

Ghost money

The likelihood of the back office being actively involved with 'ghost money' is small, since the initial contact will govern everything and this initial contact would normally be made by senior managers or dealers. Ghost money is the term given to funds which are allegedly available for investment in a large amount for a long-term fixed deposit. Various individuals will turn up with a letter purporting to confirm that they are the legal owners of funds about to mature with another reputable bank. This is evidenced by details on the headed notepaper of this other bank - but if the bank receiving these people is duped into believing this, the 'depositors' will look most reasonable by asking for a small percentage of this deposit as an advance - the deposit, of course, does not exist and the bank loses all the monies advanced.

The only way the back office comes into this is paying the funds mistakenly advanced or in seeking confirmation of the existence of the ghost money. However, strict adherence to procedures in the back office could prevent this type of situation arising. Often the fake deposit has been typed on paper created from the copying of a letter-head tossed thoughtlessly into a waste-paper basket from which a cleaner has retrieved it and passed it on to these fraudsters. Telexes or phone calls may come through to the back office and ask for confirmations of particular deposits - these should not be answered but referred to the head of department, who would need to ensure from instructions already held whether he was in a position to respond to the enquiry. Finally, there have been cases where individuals will phone in purporting to have large sums of money to invest, mostly for long-term deposits. Once again, these calls should not be treated lightly but referred to a higher authority to handle.

Data maintenance/protection

Most banks now take full advantage of the advances in information technology in order to reduce data processing costs and to increase productivity and efficiency in their daily operations. As a result, they depend heavily on the reliability of the various computer systems used across the whole gamut of tasks from accounting to payment execution. Thus the loss of a bank's computer system will have a major influence on its ability to operate. This is equally true whether the loss is from mechanical failure, power interruption or the results of a computer virus.

Thus, for each of these eventualities, a bank should have contingency plans. The most usual one would be to export the tapes to an external site so that data can be retrieved in the event of the destruction of records at the bank's address. Similarly, full contingency plans to operate from an external address - should the whole bank be destroyed - were put in place after the Irish Republican Army (IRA) attacks on London.

Internal protection of data is also crucial and this entails the secrecy required of individual passwords for access to the bank's records. Absences of authorised staff from their desks should only be allowed once access to the screen has been cleared, ie, they should sign off. Similarly, all employees should be made aware of the requirement not to divulge any information about their employer's business to anyone outside the bank. Indeed, the Data Protection Act also makes specific requirements of all people who have access to a database and have to sign to confirm that they will only use the information for the purpose for which it is intended. Any failure to observe these requirements can result in litigation.

The employer is under the obligation to make all such legal/moral compliance requirements clear to employees. Familiarisation with all such areas of compliance forms an integral part of their duties and to remain *au fait* with all changes. A different form of data maintenance is included in the need to ensure all automatic systems that generate entries/accounting data based on holidays are regularly updated so that the system does not try to send payments on invalid dates/weekends.

Finally, there is the people problem - loss of key people can mean that a situation arises with which the remaining staff are unfamiliar (such as end-of-year procedures). This latter loss of human resources could also have an influence on another due diligence procedure - the opening account procedures and checks on Memorandum and Articles to check potential *ultra vires* actions - remember Hammersmith and Fulham on IRS?

Recording of telephones

In view of the vast amounts of money which changes hands daily on the strength of word of mouth agreement, it has long been a requirement of the Bank of England that dealing rooms install recording equipment for all dealers' phones. The tapes have to be kept for two months. This practice can easily resolve any dispute on what was or was not said and is usually extended to back office phones as well. The maintenance of tapes, familiarity with the operation of the machine - especially changes to British Summer Time (BST) from Greenwich Mean Time (GMT), and security of access (regarding unauthorised alteration/blanking of tapes) all fall within back office duties (London Code of Conduct, p.7/8, s.48/49).

Security and Futures Association (SFA)

This is the regulatory body which regulates some practices in the dealing rooms. Traders who are likely to be in conversation with clients, ie, non-professionals, are required to pass examinations which prove that they know the rights of both the principal and the customer. It also gives the individual protection against any case brought against them, without which they would be personally liable rather than the bank.

The Financial Services Act/Bank of England wholesale counter-party

Clients who have dealt during the past 18 months in amounts below a specified amount (varying according to instrument) are afforded certain protection which 'professionals' are deemed not to need. It falls to the back office to keep up-to-date records of these clients and maintain them should they change with the passing of time (London Code of Conduct, p.3; p.4, s.19; p.6, s.34-37; p.8, s.51; p.15, s.107).

In larger institutions, a separate compliance section may monitor this and take the responsibility for it. All paper records are considered confidential and thus all should be shredded.

Both of the above supervisory bodies are currently being merged into the new Financial Services Authority.

CHAPTER 6

POST EMU/THE FUTURE

A survey in April 1998 by Mitchell Madison found that 85% of fund managers think there is a chance of EMU collapsing within the first five years. It is worth remembering that the Maastricht convention makes absolutely no allowance for any such contingency. (It is also significant that only 53% of the respondent to the survey had any contingency plans themselves!) Possible catalysts might be either a failure in the TARGET settlement system or the implications of the storm still brewing in the Far East and Japan. In the case of the former possibility, what would the ECB do, turn off TARGET and let interest rates float? The major concern is that there is no legal precedent for a currency unsupported by a sovereign state.

What should happen is that the combination of all the nations of EMU, with its new risk-free currency and the impact of technology in a globalised environment, should lead to greater integration of European capital markets. This in turn is expected to lead to an increased level of financial activity in a central exchange risk free situation which will increase competition, accelerate product development and change institutional and individual behaviour. In the terms of a virtuous circle this then should lead to a further move in integrating Europe's markets - another survey sees a major repatriation of assets currently held outside the EMU area by 2001.

If you want to look on the pessimistic side you might consider the following. There are 10,000 banks in Europe today. How many will we need to handle one currency? Also since banks have been dematerialising via derivative markets' interest, liquidity and credit risk, will we need any banks at all - or banks as they exist today? Technology is well on the way to replacing them - at least in their current format.

Whatever the outcome, as far as the implications for back office are concerned, each one will have to make provision for handling payment in euros. Most of the work will have to wait until the last weekend in December. This work is concerned with the conversion of all assets from the national currencies of the first 11 members of EMU into the Euro.

Conversion

Over the 1998 May holiday weekend in Britain, it was agreed at political level that the rates at which the participating currencies will be irrevocably locked from 1 January 1999 will be based on their current ERM bilateral central rates. They are set out in Table 6.1. The 'in' national central banks (NCBs) will have ensured, through appropriate market techniques, that on 31 December 1998 market exchange rates between each pair of 'in' currencies - implied by the regular concertation procedure for calculating daily official ECU rates - will equal their ERM bilateral central rates. The treaty requirement, that the adoption of the irrevocable conversion rates for the euro must not modify the external value of the ECU (which will be replaced 1:1 by the euro), will thus have been satisfied (see Appendix 9 for euro schedule).

It was not possible to announce before end-1998 the irrevocable conversion rates between each participating currency and the euro itself. This is because the ECU is a currency basket, which includes the Danish krone, the Greek drachma and sterling (which will not participate on 1 January 1999). To calculate the irrevocable conversion rates on 31 December, the regular daily concertation procedure for the official ECU will be used (see Figure 6.1).

To convert national currencies into euros, the rates will be expressed to six significant places, for example, euro = FF 6.60054 and euro = DEM 1.96804. Abbreviations to 6.60 or 1.92 are not allowed. Amounts then achieved will be rounded, thus, 2 euro = DEM 3.93608 which becomes 3.94 and 10 euro = DEM 19.6804 which becomes 19.68. Similarly, 100 euro in DEM = 100 x 1.96804 = DEM 196.80 or 100 DEM in euros would be 100/1.96804 = euro 50.811975 = euro 50.81. Inverse rates are not to be used.

Table 6.1 ERM bilateral central rates used in determining the irrevocable conversion rates for the euro.

	DM100=	BF/LF100=	SP100=	FF100=	IEP1=	ITL1000=	DFl00=	AS100=	ESC100=	FM100=
DM										
BF/LF	2062.55									
SP	8507.22	412.462								
FF	335.386	16.2608	3.94237							
IEP	40.2676	1.95232	0.473335	12.0063						
ITL	99000.2	4799.90	1163.72	29518.3	2458.56					
DF	112.674	5.46285	1.32445	33.5953	2.79812	1.13812				
AS	703.552	34.1108	8.27006	209.774	17.4719	7.10657	624.415			
ESC	10250.5	496.984	120.492	3056.34	254.560	103.541	9097.53	1456.97		
FM	304.001	14.7391	3.57345	90.6420	7.54951	3.07071	269.806	43.2094	2.96571	

Figure 6.1 Conversion between national denominations of the euro and with other currencies.

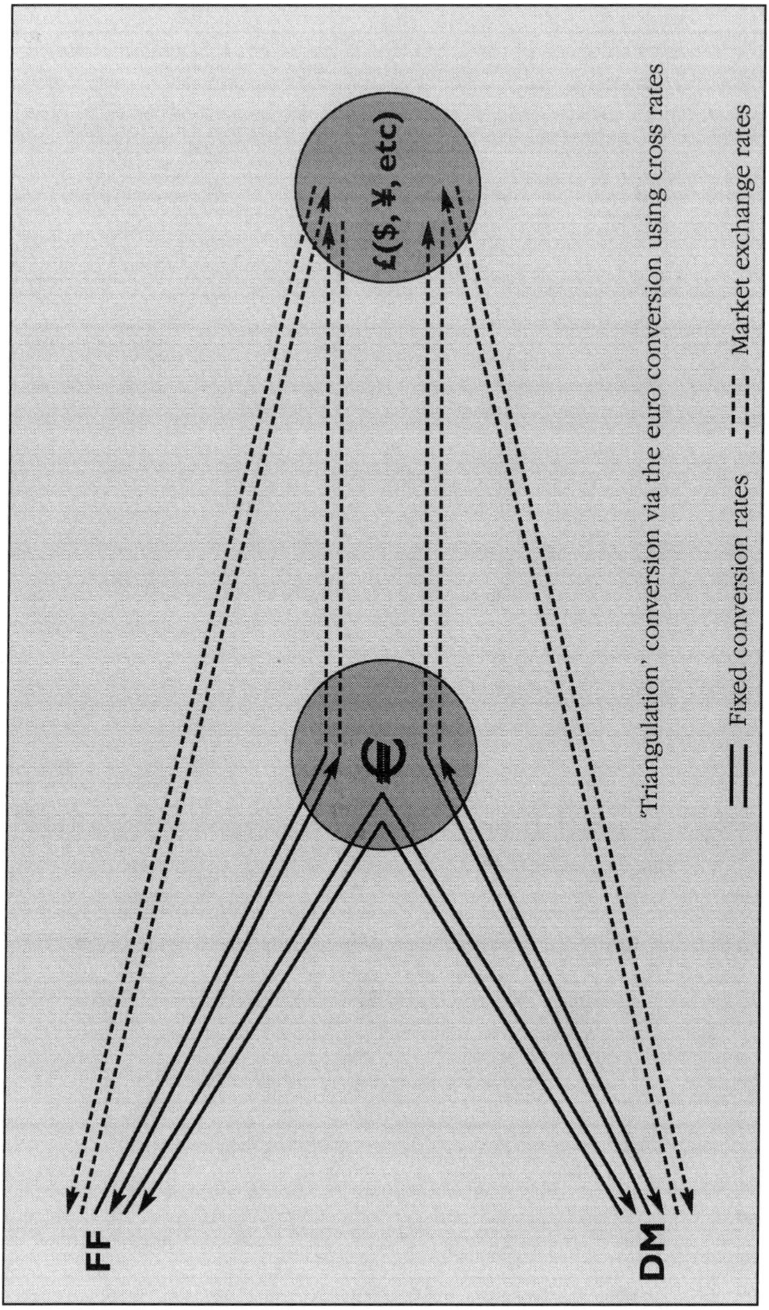

£ ($, ¥, etc)

€

FF

DM

'Triangulation' conversion via the euro conversion using cross rates

════ Fixed conversion rates   ┄┄┄ Market exchange rates

Triangulation is used to convert one national currency to another national currency, for example, 10,000 FF converted into DEM would be calculated as follows:

- FF = euro 10,000/ 6.60054 = euro 1,515.0275583.
- Round to euro 1,515.0276.
- Convert into DEM = 1,515.0276 x 1.96804 = DEM 2,981.634917 which gets rounded to 2,981.63.

Converting from 'in' currency to non participator would be calculated as follows:

If euro = GBP 0.6778 and euro = DEM 1.96804, to convert DEM 1,000 to GBP:

- Convert DEM to euro = 1,000/ 1.96804 = euro 508.119753.
- Convert intermediary amount of euro to GBP = 508.12 x .6778 = GBP 344.40376, which gets rounded to GBP 344.40.

Once all the conversion has been effected, then the euro becomes just another currency in which to deal. Obviously ahead of the changeover, new accounts in euro will have to be established, SSIs exchanged, links to TARGET established and some training of staff undertaken. Note that, since between January 1999 and the end of 2001, at the time of writing, there is still a policy of 'no compulsion, no prohibition' in the use of euros, each institution will have to negotiate with its clients over the closure of old national currency accounts - this leaves a lot of scope for confusion!

One area which will require some extra attention post EMU will be that of money laundering. The point of entry for funds emanating from a dubious source will now be much more difficult to track down. Although the various codes of conduct applied around the world make their recommendations regarding the responsibility for checking out sources - ie, with receiving bank or jointly broker and bank - any suspicion within the back office in respect of a new or unidentifiable depositor is best referred to a compliance officer or money laundering reporting officer so that the back office may rest assured that it has fulfilled its duty.

Post euro

The irrevocable conversion rates between the euro and the 11 participating countries were set on 1 January 1999 (see Table 6.2). The German method of euro conversion of government bonds is round up to nearest cent, thus

Table 6.2 Euro conversion rates.

Currency	Euro conversion rate
German marks	1.95583
French francs	6.55957
Italian lire	1936.27
Spanish pesetas	166.386
Dutch guilders	2.29371
Belgian francs	40.3399
Austrian schillings	13.7603
Portuguese escudos	200.482
Finnish markka	5.94573
Irish pounds	0.787564
Luxembourg francs	40.3399

DEM 100,000 at a conversion rate of E1=DEM 1.92573 becomes E51,928.36. Finland, Luxembourg, Belgium, Ireland, Portugal and Spain will adopt the same method. (Belgium, however, has decided to introduce a new day count basis from 1 January and will not wait till next coupon date.)

The French method is to round down to nearest whole euro. Thus FRF 100,00 OAT at a rate of E1=FRF 6.54321 becomes E15,283.00 plus a small cash compensation. The Dutch will round down to nearest whole euro.

There is still some minor disagreement about the GBP and the euro, or vice versa. 80% of the London market met with the Bank of England and the British Bankers' Association to agree the EUR/GBP. The EBS has already reached same conclusion as has the ACI. Since this does go against current practice to quote the stronger currency first, and the EUR/GBP would result in a figure less than 1, this could prove awkward, but will have to be adjusted for. Reuters look likely to quote both ways and await the market convention before it decides.

The Internet and TARGET systems which will go live with the euro bring real-time, confirmed processing within half an hour. Cedel and Euroclear are also moving to real-time settlement. The London Clearing House (LCH) is pressing ahead to launch the first clearing system for OTC derivatives, 'SwapClear', by August 1999.

Swaps

The expected outcome - for which some changes will be necessary within the back office function - for capital market transactions is the following:

- The fixed leg will be based on an annualised 30/360 day basis.
- The floating leg will be based on six-month Euribor (see below) on an actual/360 day basis.
- The payment date can be any day Monday to Friday except 25 December and 1 January (TARGET is closed).
- The fixing date will be any TARGET day two days before start date

Everything looks well prepared, providing the 1,000+ individual issues get converted in time.

The possibility for change does exist, especially regarding the fixing base. Libor has been a highly effective and respected benchmark for years and a survey (originated by Westdeutsche Landesbank in London) leaves room for those who were indifferent at the time to come down on the side of Euro Libor after all.

Further question marks relate to the new minimum amounts of trading lots, the disappearance of benchmarks and the method for trading the odd lots created through conversion. ISDA documentation does cater for the failure of new acceptable benchmarks to appear by using quotes provided by specified reference banks.

Euro Libor and Euribor

Euro Libor will be a measure of the cost of euro funds based on the offer rates quoted by 16 of the most active banks in the London market. By contrast, Euribor will be a measure of the average cost of funds over the whole euro area based on a much larger panel of banks (initially 57) and including at least one from each member state within the euro area (see Table 6.3).

Many market participants expect there to be a spread between the two rates owing to their different coverage. Euro Libor is likely to be lower than Euribor if ECB reserve requirements impose a cost on deposit-taking by banks established in the euro area. It is possible that the Euro Libor:Euribor spread will be actively traded, for example, using basis swaps.

Use of Euro Libor in the international markets will benefit from familiarity (especially among non-EU institutions), and from the liquidity that derives from the existing weight of contracts based on the current ECU and national currency Libor (which will move over to Euro Libor). In this way

Table 6.3 Alternative Euro Libor settings.

	Euro BBA Libor	**Euribor**
Panel	16 major banks active in euro markets in London.	57 banks: 47 selected by national banking associations to represent euro markets in the participating member states. 10 international 'pre-in' banks active in the euro market with an office in the euro area.
Calculation basis	Discard top and bottom 4 Average remainder	Discard top and bottom 15% Average remainder
Time of fixing	11.00 London time daily	11.00 Brussels time daily
Fixing days	All TARGET days	
For value	Second TARGET day after fixing	
Fixing periods	1 week, 1 month to 12 months	

Euro Libor will be one of the immediate beneficiaries of EMU; the notional principal of outstanding interest rate swaps in participating currencies in 1995 was some $3,767 billion, second only to US dollar outstandings of $4,372 billion.

International market participants may prefer to link new transactions to Euro Libor in order to avoid the basis risk in relation to wholesale money market positions in London and existing Libor-based assets or liabilities.

Domestic market participants in the euro area, on the other hand, may prefer to use Euribor, which will replace the national interbank rates (Fibor, Pibor, etc) and will use the same panel as the new overnight reference rate for the euro (EONIA). Marché à Terme Internationale de France (MATIF) has announced that it will adopt Euribor. Deutche Terminbörse (DTB) has announced that it will offer the market a choice, during the transition period, of Euribor and Euro Libor. LIFFE has agreed (January 1999) to use Euribor for its euro contracts.

Euro Libor may be made available on the basis of T+O as well as T+2, following current British Bankers' Association (BBA) market consultations, if there is sufficient demand.

Regulatory changes

The new Financial Services Authority came into existence in June 1998 in the UK to take over the duties of the Bank of England's banking supervision role and was expanded and renamed the Securities and Investment Board (SIB). It will also acquire the regulatory and registration functions of the self-regulating organisations (SROs), the DTI insurance directorate, the Building Societies Commission, the Friendly Societies Commission and the Registry of Friendly Societies. The schedule for the full hand-over is late 1999 - this is subject to the passing of some amendments to the Banking Act. This, no doubt will lead to some changes in the reporting required (see *Financial Services Authority: an outline*, published 1997, reprinted May 1998).

The major concern is that a single body suffers from the same problem as EMU, ie, the 'one size fits all' theory. A single ombudsman will be addressing all the various problems of the nature of a Barings collapse, the Maxwell scandal, the Roger Levitt case, the various crises at Lloyds of London and the massive pension debacle - although with all that, the size of banking losses over the last 25 years is miniscule compared to the same area of losses in the USA.

Additionally, it was announced in August 1998 that the capital adequacy requirements, first promulgated by the BIS in 1988, are to be revised. This again will have implications for all the data currently provided via back office for the VaR calculations. New percentages reflecting the relative risk between exposures to an OECD government compared to a normal commercial name are likely to be the major changes

New instruments

This remains favourite to be the largest source of concern for the back office role. As further mergers take place amongst the financial community polarising further the level of activity of the top 20/30 banks and the rest, these larger institutions will inevitably put their minds to new ways of trading.

Whilst this would initially only put the onus on the bigger banks' back offices, it will not be long before the other tiers of banks are required by their niche client to at least account for them if not actively market make in them.

The particular area of rapid expansion at this time is in credit derivatives (see Bank of England Banking Act Report 1996/7, pp. 32/33 and *Euromoney*, December 1996, p. 81 et seq), which is a type of insurance offered to protect an exposure just to the risk that the counterparty fails or is sufficiently adversely affected by some occurrence to affect its credit standing. These fall into three categories - the total return swap, the credit spread and the default spread.

CHAPTER 7

RISK

We now come to the real implications of the word 'beyond' in this book's title. As emphasised throughout, with the best will in the world, the roles carried out by the back office itself could be the source of some of the eventual risk that is being run by any institution. This comes under the category of operational risk. So what we need to examine further are what constitutes operational risk *beyond* that which we have so far explored.

Operational/technological risk

This risk encompasses everything that can go wrong with the processing procedure. Our reliance on technology is absolute. If one follows the chain of processing systems through the cycle it becomes apparent that not only are there a myriad of systems controlling the reporting and processing function within your own organisations, but also that banks are reliant on international clearing and payment systems, ie, CHIPS and CHAPS, and the processing systems of your counterparty. Add in external information providers, such as Reuters and Bloomberg, and regulatory reporting systems, such as TRAX, and it becomes very apparent that banks, particularly trading rooms, are driven by technology and also the need to remain state of the art.

System failure is now the great concern of banks. It is no longer acceptable or possible to treat long-term loss of functionality as something that can be sorted out at the home of the general manager or head trader. Contingency planning has become big business. Terrorism and incidents like the hurricane of 1987 have focused the attention of financial institutions. All systems must be fully backed up, duplicated and, if possible, be available immediately in the event of a disaster. Banks now plan on the loss of premises through terrorism, fire, etc, and how quickly they can get back into full business from nothing. The aim is under 48 hours.

At the other end of the spectrum is human error. Whilst systems are designed to help the user in automating many of the repetitions in processing there always remains the risk that incorrect payment instructions or mis-keying leads to interest penalty claims. Operational managers are now beginning to implement controls based on performance levels (benchmarking) that help identify the weaknesses in processing systems. Operations departments are being asked to sign service level agreements with their respective front offices.

Some factors which impact on risk management are outside the direct control of the institution itself or its back office, most of that risk is down to external influences. Of these the major risk, both in terms of likelihood and actual impact, is settlement risk (see Figure 7.1).

Settlement risk

How can one define settlement risk? In the course of business there will come a specific date, as defined by the relevant contract, where Counterparty A must pay Counterparty B in settlement of a transaction. It is the receiving party that takes the risk of non-receipt. If he does not receive payment then he is out of pocket for the full amount of the payment or 100% of the nominal value of the contract or the agreed margin in the case of a derivative contract. This is called the credit risk dimension of settlement risk.

Instrument types that incur counterparty settlement risk at maturity include:

- FX spot - each counterparty will be expecting settlement from each other.
- Maturing FX forward contracts - becomes a spot contract two days prior to maturity.
- Any free Eurobond settlement - ie, between different custodians or nostros (not Euroclear and Cedel).
- The payment of margin or fees in relation to futures contracts or FRAs.
- Option premiums.
- Transfers of payment on interest rate or currency swaps.

Figure 7.1 Today' trading process - where's the risk?

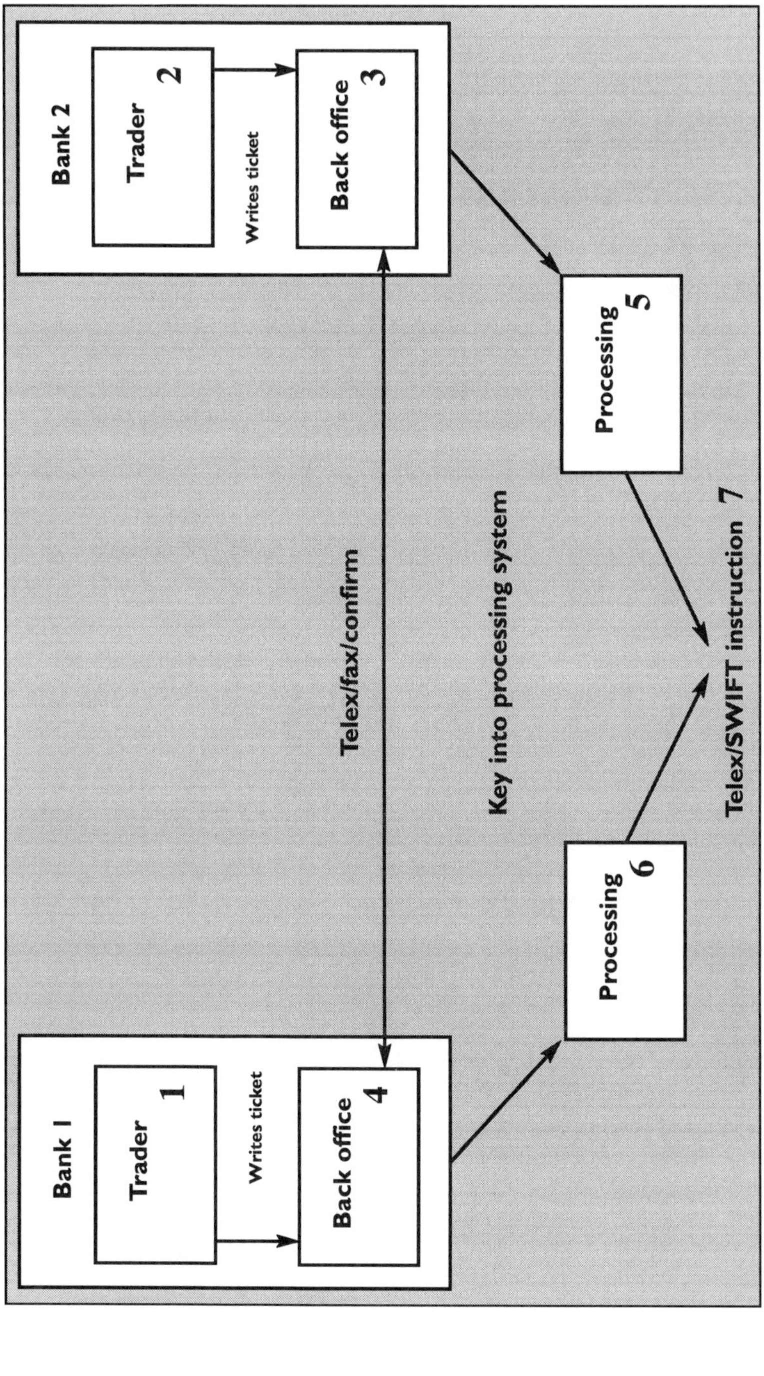

Whilst we consider the counterparty and set limits that reflect the total amount of payments to be received on any particular day from him, by far the majority of non-receipt of funds are owing to human/system errors. They typically represent:

- Dealers writing incorrect details on the ticket.
- System failure.
- Incorrect checking of confirmations by back office.

The aspect of most concern in settlement risk, particularly in the FX market, is the risk of releasing payment before confirmation of receipt of the incoming funds has been received. Think of the UK bank who has sold yen against US dollars. To make payment in yen he will have to release his payment instruction two days prior to the settlement date. Japan is closed as the UK opens for same value, and the banks require the payment instructions the day before settlement. The US dollar receipt will not be advised until the morning after the settlement date. The US closes at 8 pm UK time, when hopefully most of us have gone home. This is known as Herstatt risk (see page 34 and Figure 7.2).

Herstatt risk
The Committee on Payment and Settlement Systems (CPSS) of the G-10 Central Banks has advanced a case for assessing settlement risk to be equal to in aggregate to a multiple of the average daily FX turnover figure reported by the BIS. It even thinks that a bank's maximum FX/settlement exposure could equal or even surpass the amount receivable for three days' worth of trades. This could amount to a figure for any one counterparty which exceeds the bank's entire capital.

The collapses of the US investment bank, Drexel Burnham Lambert, in 1990, BCCI in 1991 and Barings in 1995 are excellent case studies for this type of risk. The amount at risk equals the full amount of currency purchased and lasts from the time that a payment currency (for the currency sold) can no longer be cancelled unilaterally until the time the currency purchased is received with finality (irrevocable and unconditional).

The Noel Report of 1993 assumes the fundamental concept that multi-currency DVP is assured. This means that the final transfer of one asset only occurs if, and only if, the final transfer of another asset occurs.

In June 1998 the SWIFT US National Group released a set of recommendations to improve market practices in respect of cancellations and recon-

Figure 7.2 Cross currency settlement risk (Herstatt, 1974).

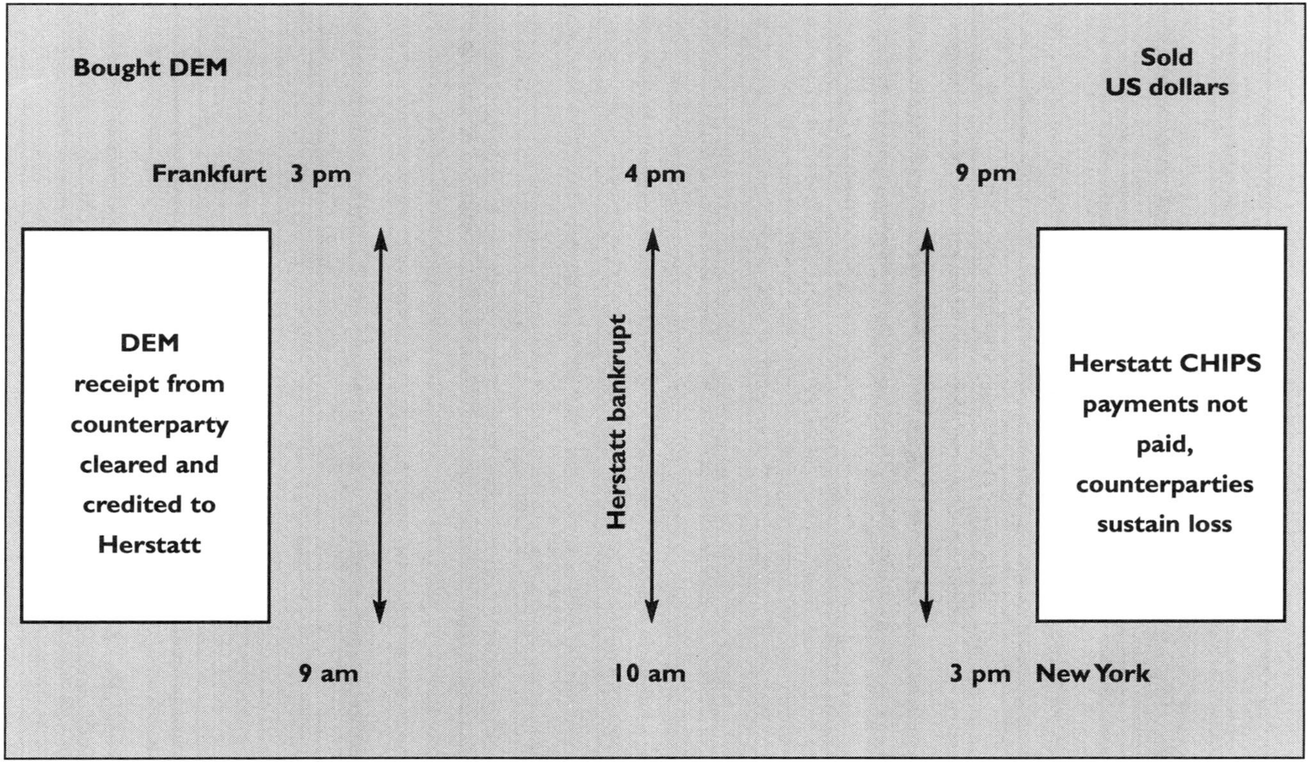

Bought DEM

Sold US dollars

Frankfurt 3 pm

4 pm

9 pm

9 am

10 am

3 pm New York

Herstatt bankrupt

DEM receipt from counterparty cleared and credited to Herstatt

Herstatt CHIPS payments not paid, counterparties sustain loss

ciliations of FX transaction thereby reducing interbank settlement exposure and decreasing FX settlement risk. The report suggested that the required reduction in risk profile can be achieved through improvements to back office processing, correspondent banking arrangements, netting capabilities and risk management controls. Thus it should be anticipated that the back office will have new and additional demands made of it in the coming months/years.

One way is to secure the agreement on an industry level by setting rules and creating service level agreements for FX nostro banks. This was formalised in April 1998 under a paper called *RISE*. This report recommends that:

- The cancellation deadline should be no more than two hours before the corresponding clearing system's opening.
- All credit advice messages should be sent within 10 minutes of receipt of the credit from CHIPS, Fedwire or other clearing systems.
- Beneficiary banks should have the ability to reconcile within two hours of the closing time.
- Final reconciliation should be within 30 minutes of the closing time of the latest local payments system.
- Banks using MT 210s should reconcile within two hours of the closing time.
- Banks should use SSIs as a default.

Whilst a considerable number of the decisions on the above will be individual choices, any changes will - once again - end up as back office primary responsibilities.

The authorities are also concerned with systemic and liquidity risk. *Liquidity risk* envisages the scenario where the availability of a currency or instrument becomes nil or there is no longer a market and settlement cannot be made. Examples of this situation include currencies becoming non convertible. *Systemic risk* is where there is a concern that the inability of a financial institution to make payment or settle a contract will cause its counterparty to fail, and there becomes a knock-on effect throughout the international markets.

Other external sources of risk - again totally outside any individual institution's control - then are limited to *legal risk*.

Legal risk

Whilst this includes documentation and the risk of claims made against a defaulting client through the courts, it also includes the legal status of companies/corporates to enter into various types of transactions. Hammersmith & Fulham was deemed to have illegally entered into derivative transactions, consequently banks were unable to claim against the authority for losses made as H&M had conducted transactions outside its powers (*ultra vires*).

The regulatory structure in the UK, through the SIB including the SFA and The Bank of England, sets strict rules in relation to how business is to be undertaken. It is each bank's responsibility to ensure that it has in place procedures that ensure sensitive information is managed responsibly on a need to know basis.

Political risk

In some parts of the world the instability of the political regime causes concern. The fact that governments can, through policy and military takeovers, effectively change the business structure of a country and directly cause losses to existing positions and/or portfolios is clear risk. Banks will set country limits, which control the level of exposure they are prepared to take in a particular country. It is likely that the USA or G7 type economies will have unlimited exposure yet some of the African countries can not even be described as emerging. It is unlikely that banks will want to engage in high levels of exposure in these types of countries.

Adverse publicity risk

Financial institutions hate bad publicity. It can, in the worst case, bring a company to its knees. Irving Trust was a US bank that sacked one of its employees from the IT department. This person promptly hacked back into Irving's money transfer system. He did not steal money, instead he made public what he had done. Customers were extremely concerned about this lack of security and promptly moved their accounts to another bank.

Fraud

Financial institutions also need to protect themselves from fraud both internally and externally. International action through the Financial Action Task Force (a committee set up by 26 member countries) continues the war against money launderers. Banks need to be vigilant for fraudulent or counterfeit documents presented for payment. Another very common type of fraud is through internal theft and is usually for relatively small amounts.

Market risk

This does not exhaust the total sources of risk, in fact it leaves us still with the major one that applies to all front office operations - market risk. Even though back office does not create this risk or assumes prime responsibility for its monitoring, many of the controls that can be exercised to reduce/monitor/minimise such risk will often fall within the duties of some part of the 'support' or back office function. It is a very real risk and one which, with the appropriate level of co-operation and care between all interested parties, can be actively managed and kept within bounds.

Market risk involves determining the sensitivity of a currency/instrument to changes in the financial markets and assessing the extent of the exposure to the risks of such changes. The risk must be measured across the entire portfolio of currencies and instruments. Given the size and diversity of some investment banks' trading portfolios this is not an inconsiderable task. Let's look firstly at foreign exchange and where the risks derive.

FX spot

Currency mismatching of one currency varies in value against another. All convertible currencies are valued against the US$ (world trade is conducted in US$). The calculation of cross rates are worked through the dollar equivalent of both currencies. The value of one currency may therefore change in relation to the US$ owing to economic pressures or political influences that are specific to that currency.

The price at which each currency is bought or held will inevitably change throughout the day and certainly overnight as it is traded internationally and has no respect for time zones. A client places a large order with a bank, which is accepted. In an extreme case the order may mean that the FX spot desk is holding a very large position (long or short) until it has managed to cover the position in the market. Large buyers or sellers can change the market price. It is likely that the position can only be offloaded in bits. It is conceivable that the price may move against the original cost of the order whilst the bank goes about clearing the position. The head trader must have been aware of this intraday risk and factored this into his or her decision to accept the order.

Overnight risk reflects any price movement against the average price of any net position held overnight. In the morning the trader could arrive to see adverse movements in rates internationally that have altered the current value of his position.

FX forwards

Movements in forward foreign exchange rates are dictated by movements in relative interest rates. Forward rates are calculated using the respective interest rate for that currency for like periods. Consequently a six-month forward CHF price and the six-month USD interbank will reflect the six-month CHF interbank rates in the same market place. It therefore follows that any change in interest rates will have an impact on the forward price. Forward positions therefore are subject to not only currency risks but also interest rate risk (see interest rate risk below).

In setting realistic trading limits for forwards it is essential to have an accurate method of quantifying the level of risk (the worst case loss) in the event of extreme price fluctuations. The risk is normally expressed as a percentage of a currency position and limits are set accordingly. Because US dollars are viewed as a relatively stable currency, a larger forward position than say a forward position in Argentinean pesos which is a more volatile currency, may be allowed. The limits and level of risk to be taken will always be judgemental, what counts is accurately identifying and measuring the risk (see value at risk discussed on page 94).

It is worth saying something about arbitrage. On occasions there may arise an interest rate differential between currencies that does not accurately reflect the respective forward prices. In other words, purchasing another currency forward may be advantageous because the cost of converting may be cheaper or the interest rate cost less. Identifying any such trading opportunities is called arbitrage. In an efficient market these windows of opportunity do not last long. Market forces will bring the rates into line and the window will close.

Interest rate risk

Interest rate risk can be defined as the exposure of a bank's financial condition to adverse changes in interest rates. As an excessive interest rate risk can be a significant threat to the bank's earnings and capital base, sound risk management systems are required. Limits need to be realistic and the methodology of calculating risk accurate in order for exposure to be kept within realistic levels.

Gap risk/repricing risk

This is the most widely understood type of interest rate risk. It arises from timing differences in maturities and the repricing process.

The example used in Chapter 1 to describe risk diversification can also be used to identify the unhedged risk created by funding a fixed rate loan against short-term deposit on a repricing basis.

A bank loan US$10m for one year at 6% is funded by a three-month deposit at 5.5%. If, at the end of three months, interest rates have risen to say 6.5% the margin has moved from a profitable situation to one that will post losses to the P&L. The cash flows on the loan are fixed over its lifetime, while interest paid on the funding is variable and, in this example, has increased after the short-term deposit matures.

Yield curve risk

What does the yield curve represent? It reflects the economic value of interest rate instruments which include bonds and the money markets. The economic value can be defined as the current value of future cash flows. A 10-year fixed rate bond halfway through its term is unlikely to be valued at par owing to rate changes since inception, the shortened maturity profile, and the remaining coupon payments. The yield curve therefore reflects the time value of money. The classic yield curve shape shows short-term rates lower than long-term rates in a gradual arc upwards over time. On occasions the curve can become flat (where short-term rates and long-term rates are the same) or inverted (where short-term rates are higher than long-term rates). Usually for curves to become flat or inverted, local government monetary policy is influencing the market.

Yield curve risk occurs when anticipated shifts of the yield curve have adverse effects on a bank's income or underlying economic value. For instance, the economic value in a short position in 10-year government bonds hedged by a long position in 5-year government notes could decline sharply if the yield curve steepens, even if the position is hedged against parallel movements in the yield curve.

We have seen the relationship between the FX forward rate and interest rates. Whilst the changes in value between different currencies has an impact on the forward rate, changes in interest rates also have an impact through mismatched positions and yield curve risk. Other related products that are influenced by interest rate risk are forward rate agreements (which are hedging instruments), interest rate futures and interest rate swaps.

Basis risk
Another important source of risk arises from the imperfect correlation in the adjustment of rates earned and paid on different instruments with otherwise similar repricing characteristics. Cash (or the underlying) markets may not move at the same speed as a derivative, eg, if a one-year loan that is renewed monthly based on Libor is hedged by a deposit that reprices monthly but based on the US treasury bill rate there may be spread changes as the two index rates move closer or apart.

Correlation risk

This reflects the risk emanating from instruments that can be matched through similar or opposite price correlations, and can be used as an offset against each other. They need not be of similar repricing or market types. For example, the US$/DEM rate had similar price characteristics as the US$/NLG (Netherlands guilders) as both currencies were economically tied through the ERM. As both rates will tend to move in the same direction it is noted that the rates are positively correlated and a long position in one currency will be offset by a short position in the other.

Equally in some instances the price movement of a currency or instrument may be matched by an instrument that moves in the opposite way. This is known as *negative correlation* and therefore two long positions can be offset against each other. If there is no correlation between rates either positively or negatively, then no offset can be achieved. This is called nil correlation.

Replacement risk

Let's look at an example:
We buy GBP 1,000,000 @ 1.65 for USD 1,650,000 value 6 months. After 3 months, the client goes bankrupt (3-month forward FX rates are @ 1.75).

Replacement cost of contract:
GBP 1,000,000 will cost USD 1,750,000.

Result: If the customer cannot deliver and defaults on the contract we must cover our new exposure on the market at a potential loss of USD 100,000.

If your counterparty declares bankruptcy before the settlement of forward or off balance sheet type transactions then, assuming a hedged position, the transaction must be replaced in the market. It is unlikely that this can be done at the existing rate as rates will have changed and you will need to replace the transaction for a shorter period than the original contract. The risk is that the rates will have moved adversely and there is a loss to book. As in all cases of risk measurement you must assume worst case.

Firstly it becomes apparent that replacement is measured against the individual transaction and not against a portfolio of trades that is the case with market risk. With each counterparty it is possible to have facilities for several product types, eg, FX spot (or settlement limits), FX forwards, interbank loans, IRS and fixed income trading. Each product type will be measured and analysed against historical volatility models.

CHAPTER 8

▌▌▌

RISK MANAGEMENT

Although the source of the risk will always be initiated by the front office, to a large extent, the back office (or maybe middle office) will be instrumental in assisting in the whole process. Many of the duties that have been covered in the earlier chapters themselves - provided they are carried out efficiently - lessen the risk profile. However, in most instances the back office will only be involved after the risk has already been assumed. It is with the front office risk that we will now concentrate.

As touched upon earlier, although it would be theoretically possible for additional external controls to be implemented to control the management of risk, the cost, intrusiveness and acceptance make it impractical after all. However, it is not beyond the realms of possibility for the central authorities to lay the ground rules which the internal controls should then encompass.

Major losses resulting from poor quality loans both by sector and geographical location, led to the establishment of the Cooke Committee which eventually brought out the 8% capital requirement in 1987. Since that time, other market losses have led the central authorities to extend their recommendations beyond those of the maintenance of the statutory 8% capital to the requirement to risk weight and correlate the whole portfolio of an institution to arrive at the concept of the maximum risk reflected in one number - VaR - value at risk.

Recent developments

On the basis of the crises that arose in Asia, leading central banks - led by the US Federal Reserve - have raised concerns concerning the IMF's proposal to set its own 'code of conduct'. The main objection is that the IMF draft rules seem to be set to suit itself, whilst an additional concern is that, extending these rules to cover payment systems, is seen as going too far. The BIS looks likely to broker a deal where the IMF will have the responsibility to produce the code but with individual central bank views taken into account.

This concern is not confined to the IMF document. In the UK, the City has expressed major reservations about the scope of the new Financial Services Authority. Concerns have been expressed on such matters as accountability, appeals procedures, the definition of market abuse and the need to distinguish between retail and wholesale markets. Depending on the outcome, some - if not the majority of the changes here - will devolve upon the back office function.

The main area which is likely to require amendment is the definition of market abuse. This needs clarification regarding the description of market abuse concerning artificial transactions which give the market the wrong impression of supply and demand market squeezes, where a single player temporarily controls an instrument and thus its price and finally the use of privileged information. Whilst the initial decision would be taken by the front office, there would be a natural spin-off for the back office to draw the attention of senior management - via its separate reporting line - of any 'unusual' practices.

Accountants have also taken fright at the results of the Asian crisis and look likely to move to using 'International Accounting Standards'. Specific matters covered would be:

- Related party lending and borrowing.
- Losses arising from foreign currency debt.
- Derivative financial instruments.
- Reporting by financial sector.
- Contingent liabilities.

A recent report showed that, of 73 banks surveyed in Korea, Thailand, Indonesia, Malaysia and the Philippines, only 25% disclose 'receivables' from associate companies; only 34% reported inter-company loans and deposits; none declared the company's risk management policy; just 19% declared foreign currency profit and losses accurately; 1% only disclosed their risks associated with derivatives and less than a third of all companies described their business by market sector.

The relevance of any new demands here on back office would be extra vigilance required on counterparties in any of these geographical areas regarding confirmations, changes in activity or acceptance of non-market pricing or additional exposure created by the front office itself to counterparties in this region.

Amendment to the Capital Accord

In April 1995 the Basle Committee on Banking Supervision issued a paper for applying capital charges to market risks incurred by banks. These risks can be defined as the risk of losses in on and off balance sheet positions arising from movements in market prices. The instruments covered by the proposed framework are the trading book of debt and equity and related off balance sheet contracts, and foreign exchange and commodity risks. These proposals were accepted and were implemented by the G10 authorities at the end of 1997.

Asset liability risk management methodology

The simplest techniques for measuring a bank's interest rate exposure is to allocate interest sensitive assets and liabilities and related off balance sheet positions into a certain number of predefined time bands according to their maturity. If fixed rate, until maturity; if floating rate, until their next repricing. Assets or liabilities lacking a definitive maturity, for example, demand deposit accounts (DDA) or savings accounts, are assigned to repricing bands based on the judgement and past experience of the bank.

Gap analysis
Using the time band allocation, assets and liabilities can be netted, in accordance with their maturity bands, to produce a repricing 'gap' for that time band. This gap can be multiplied by an assumed change in interest rates to yield an approximation of the change in net interest income that would result from such an interest rate movement. The size of the interest rate movement used can be based on a variety of factors, including historical data, estimates of future rate movements and internal judgements.

A negative gap occurs when liabilities exceed assets (including off balance sheet positions). If an increase in interest rates occurs then there would be a decline in net interest income. Conversely a positive or asset sensitive gap implies the bank's net interest income could decline if there was a decrease in the level of interest rates.

This approach, however, does have a number of shortcomings that results in the approximation of the true risk. Gap analysis does not take into account the variation in characteristics in the different instruments within each time band. They are assumed to mature or reprice simultaneously. Gap analysis also ignores the differences in spreads between interest rates that could arise through basis risk. Finally, it does not take into account any changes in the timing of payments that may occur as a result of changes in the interest rate environment, ie, exercising American OTC interest rate options or time options.

Duration analysis

This relates to yield curve risk. Simply put, duration analysis measures changes in economic value resulting from a percentage change of interest rates under the assumption that changes in value are proportional to changes in the level of interest rates, and the timing of payments is fixed. By applying sensitivity weights to each time band, the effects of changing interest rates can be evaluated. Here we look at the estimated duration of the asset/liability rather than the precise maturity/repricing date.

Used in combination with the maturity/repricing schedule, the duration weighted gaps are aggregated across time bands to produce an estimate of the change in the economic value of the bank. Banks can, by using a precise duration of each asset/liability, determine a net position for each asset/liability more accurately. An alternative approach would be to design risk weights on the basis of actual percentage changes of hypothetical instruments for each time band, as opposed to the interest rate gap profile. This approach, 'effective duration', would better capture the non-linearity of price movements arising from significant changes in market interest rates.

Simulation approaches

Many of the larger, more sophisticated banks employ more complex interest rate measurement systems. The simulation techniques include more detailed assessments of the potential effects in interest rate earnings. This involves a more detailed breakdown of the various categories on and off the balance sheet. This allows for specific assumptions about the interest and principal payments, and non-interest income and expense arising from each type of position can be incorporated. Sensitivity analysis can also be developed by incorporating more varied and refined changes in the interest rate environment. This includes changes to the slope and shape of the yield curve.

A dynamic simulation looks at changes in the bank's interest rate policy and strategy. This would quantify the risks of such changes in policy. In any risk evaluation system, be it sophisticated or not, the accuracy of the underlying information is essential for an effective and accurate risk management process.

Counterparty risk management methodology

Payment netting

One of the most effective ways of reducing settlement risk is the netting of payments between trading counterparties. Payment netting is defined as the arrangement between two counterparties to net all payments in a single currency owed between them on a given value date. The payments will be aggregated to arrive at a single currency obligation for each currency payable between the parties. The parties calculate net payments at an agreed time (usually the day before value).

Netting of payments between two counterparties (most actively used between counterparties in foreign exchange markets but can be used for many products where payments are to be made in the same currency) is known as bilateral settlement netting.

Netting arrangements are encouraged by the central authorities and have an obvious benefit to those parties involved, ie:

- The number of payments in progress and volume in transit is dramatically reduced.
- The opportunity for errors are reduced as 'human' error is largely excluded.
- Reconciliation is easier.
- Charges - when incurred - are likely to be smaller.

Against that, one has to weigh the cost of the initial set-up of netting - hardware and software - and recognise that the mere agreement of a net position between counterparties does not totally eliminate risk. For there is no guarantee that netted payments by both parties will be simultaneous, thus delivery risk may still apply.

How in practice would the various netting systems assist? We have seen in the earlier chapter the description of each variation - what is the practical application?

Netting by novation

Novation netting entails that for each value date and for each currency the parties agree that all existing contracts will be cancelled and simultaneously replaced by a new contract that aggregates and nets all of the payment obligations of the previous contacts. Novation netting is arranged when a contract is entered into and not at settlement. On settlement date, however, no difference exists between the amounts that would be calculated under novation versus the amounts calculated under payment netting. In circumstances that involve bankruptcy, novation removes selective settlement by the liquidator of the bankrupt company, ie, settling the most profitable contracts.

Netting +

This is a recently proposed technique to further reduce bilateral settlement exposures. By using Tom/next FX swaps two counterparties can offset an existing currency payment obligation just prior to settlement and roll the position to the next day, for example:

Party A owes DEM 500 to Party B, value 2 December.
Party B owes USD 322 to Party A, value 2 December.

Netting + creates a new Tom/next swap reversing the DEM flow for the same value 2 December, with a new transaction value 3 December.

Party B sells Party A DEM 500 (thus cancelling the DEM payment).
Party A buys USD, which at current market rates only equals $320 (leaving the difference of USD 2 to be settled).
Party A sells DEM 500 to Party B, value 3 December.

The counterparties must agree a source and time for setting rates and a cut-off time for calculating the amounts to be swapped and the currencies to be settled via netting+.

The details can be documented as an amendment to a master agreement or by an operational letter.

The benefits of netting + are as follows:

- It eliminates settlement risk because no capital amounts are transferred.
- No collateral is required.
- There is no counterparty substitution, third party or membership criteria.
- It can be a manual process or it can be automated.

Note - in practice, netting+ has not proved popular.

Multilateral netting

Multilateral netting is a group of banks agreeing to net their payment obligations.

Example

Bank A buys DEM 100, sells USD 99 with Bank B.
Bank A sells DEM 85, buys USD 85 with Bank C.
Bank B buys DEM 75 and sells USD 74 with Bank C.

The effect on each bank's positions is shown in Table 8.1.

In this example Banks A, B and C do one trade with each other which, with a bilateral arrangement, would leave settlement unchanged from a gross position. On a multilateral basis, however, when banks can net across all their counterparties the resulting positions are lower. In this example the total payments under a bilateral netting arrangement would total USD 516, under a multilateral arrangement the figure is reduced to USD 50.

Close-out netting

This form of netting is effectively a credit risk management tool in the event of default by a party to a trading contract. In this case the non-defaulting party has the legal right to liquidate and set off all outstanding transactions between parties. The terms of close-out are agreed between the parties including the timing and pricing methodology. Close-out netting is the calculation of the replacement cost of each transaction to the non-defaulting counterparty, converted to an agreed single currency and netted.

Let's look at an example:

Contract 1 - ABC Bank sells USD 5 million against CHF 7,303,000, value 5 September at 1.4606 with XYZ Bank.

Table 8.1 A multilateral position.

Trades and positions	Bank A		Bank B		Bank C	
	DEM	USD	DEM	USD	DEM	USD
Example trades						
1.	100	(99)	(100)	99		
2.	(85)	85			85	(85)
3.			75	(74)	(75)	74
Notional bilateral positions vs. counterparty						
Bank A			(100)	99	85	(85)
Bank B	100	(99)			(75)	74
Bank C	(85)	85	75	(74)		
Multilateral positions	15	(14)	(25)	25	10	(11)

Contract 2 - ABC Bank sells JPY 1 billion against USD 10,277,492, value 18 September at 97.3 with XYZ Bank.

Contract 3 - ABC Bank sells USD 5 million against CAD 5,990,000, value 3 October at 1.1980 with XYZ Bank.

Contract 4 - ABC Bank sells GBP 5 million against USD 7,763000, value 6 October at 1.5526 with XYZ Bank.

Let's assume that XYZ Bank defaults on 3 September, before these contracts mature. ABC Bank under the terms of its contract with XYZ Bank can calculate the replacement cost of the above contracts. The replacement value is defined as the amount that would have to be paid to enter into a contract having the same economic value as the original contract. ABC has to enter into contracts that are equal and offsetting to the original contracts for the same value dates as the original contracts.

Contract 1 - The CHF has appreciated against the USD to 1.43. ABC will need to sell CHF 7,150,000 to buy back USD 5 million.

CHF 7,303,000
− 7,150,000

CHF 153,000/1.43 = USD 106,993

Contract 2 - The JPY has appreciated to 96.5. ABC will need to sell USD 10,362,694 to buy back JPY 1 billion.

USD 10,277,492
− 10,362,694

USD − 85,202

Contract 3 - The Swiss franc has appreciated against the USD to 1.17. ABC will now need to sell CAD 5,850,000 to buy back USD 5 million.

CAD 5,990,000
− 5,850,000

CAD 140,000/1.17 = USD 119,658

Contract 4 - GBP has appreciated against the USD to 1.57. ABC will now need to sell USD 7,850,000 to buy back GBP 5 million.

US 7,763,000
− 7,850,000

US − 87,000

In order to arrive at the replacement value of each contract, the amounts are then discounted to present value (assuming a discount rate of 6%). The net positive and negative replacement values are netted to a single close-out amount *due to* ABC from XYZ.

Contract 1   + 106,957
Contract 2   − 84,989
Contract 3   + 119,062
Contract 4   − 86,524

+ 54,506

ABC Bank therefore has only USD 54,506 in credit risk to XYZ bank at the time of default. Without the benefit of close-out netting, ABC would have USD 226,019 at risk, in other words, the sum of the contracts that yielded ABC a profit after close-out.

Legal documentation

The most widely used and internationally accepted form of documentation is the ISDA master agreement. ISDA, International Swap & Derivative Association Inc, (see Figure 8.1) supports a bilateral agreement for settlement in the following products:

- Interest rate and currency swaps.
- Foreign exchange settlement.
- The exercising of OTC options including currency options.

The agreement allows for early termination and close-out netting. The agreement is binding and supported internationally. It is accepted by all major banks operating in the underlying and derivative markets.

Modern risk management methodologies

Value at risk

It is said that when Dennis Weatherstone was Chairman of JP Morgan he demanded a daily report that summarised the company's exposure to moves in the markets and provided a decent estimate of potential losses over the next 24 hours. The result became the famous '4.15 report' delivered at that time to his office. This type of reporting which tries to identify the potential losses based on trading positions has become a regulatory requirement brought about by the fear of collapse through irresponsible trading.

The purpose of value at risk (VaR) is to give an estimate of losses over a short period under 'normal' market conditions. It will not tell you what might happen during a market crash. For that, stress testing and scenario analysis are necessary. Also it does not inform you of traders entering false positions (Barings being a prime example) so there must be sound operational and technical controls that help stop misuse of limits and unauthorised trading.

Once all the data has been centralised (from various trading books, other offices, etc), the overall risk has to be calculated by aggregating the risks from individual contracts across the whole portfolio. This is done by working out the effects of moves in individual risk factors (eg, stock index, a specific point on the yield curve or swap curve, or an FX or commodity price) across the portfolio. The portfolio itself will involve large numbers of currencies and asset classes. VaR is worked out from the relationships

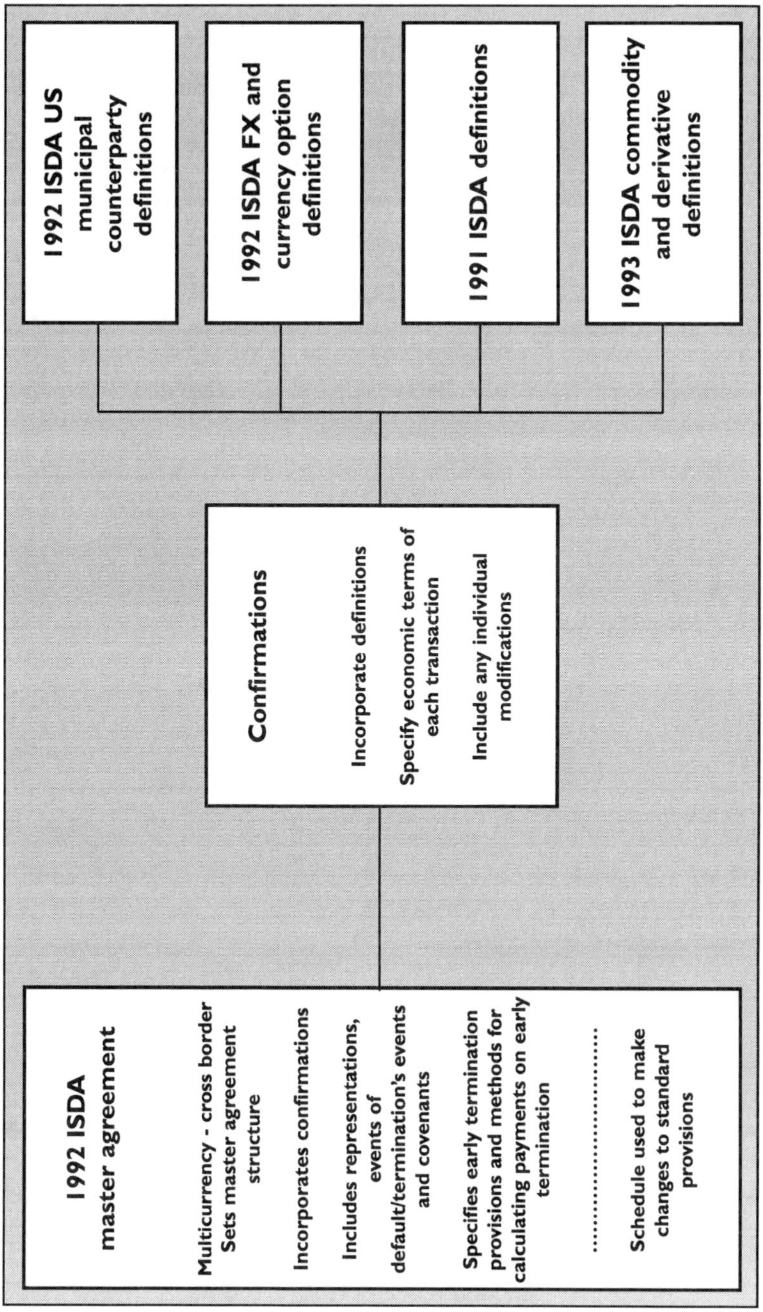

Figure 8.1 1992 ISDA documentation architecture.

1992 ISDA US municipal counterparty definitions

1992 ISDA FX and currency option definitions

1991 ISDA definitions

1993 ISDA commodity and derivative definitions

Confirmations

Incorporate definitions

Specify economic terms of each transaction

Include any individual modifications

1992 ISDA master agreement

Multicurrency - cross border Sets master agreement structure

Incorporates confirmations

Includes representations, events of default/termination's events and covenants

Specifies early termination provisions and methods for calculating payments on early termination

Schedule used to make changes to standard provisions

between the individual risk factors and the effect on the portfolio of moves in each risk factor. The potential move in each risk factor has to be inferred from past price movements. For regulatory purposes the historical price movement for assessment must reflect at least one year's data, or reflect daily market movements over the previous year. This is a huge amount of data to manage for some of the smaller institutions, however JP Morgan has been distributing its data for VaR calculations free of charge.

The basis upon which VaR is calculated has been compared and contrasted and put under the microscope. A more precise definition has emerged: 'VaR is the maximum loss that will be incurred on the portfolio with a given level of confidence over a specified holding period, based on the distribution of price changes over a given historical observation period.'

The BIS rules, known as the Basle Capital Accord, specify:

- A 99% confidence interval (ie, actual losses on the portfolio should exceed the VaR estimate not more than once every 100 days).
- A holding period of 10 days (assumes the portfolio remains unchanged for 10 days).
- A historical observation period of at least one year.

The main assumption underpinning VaR is that future price changes will be similar to past price changes upon which the risks are measured. Critics have said this is akin to driving a car by looking in the rear view mirror. It is, however, viewed as a useful tool for day-to-day risk management if it is understood that it reflects normal market conditions.

The three popular methods of calculating VaR are:

- The covariance method.
- Historic volatility.
- Monte Carlo simulation method.

The covariance method (or correlation method)

The covariance method assumes the returns on risk factors are normally distributed, the correlations between risk factors are constant and the delta (or price sensitivity to changes in a risk factor) of each portfolio constituent is constant.

To calculate VaR the volatility of each risk factor is extracted from the historical observation period. The potential effect of each component of the portfolio on the overall portfolio is worked out from the component's delta and that is the risk factor's volatility. These effects are then aggregated across the whole portfolio using the correlations between the risk factors to give the overall volatility of the portfolio value. The desired confidence interval for VaR can then be determined.

Historic volatility

Simple historic volatility is simple, however the effects of a large one-off market move can significantly distort volatilities over the forecasting period. For example, if using a 30-day historic volatility any market shock will stay in these figures for 30 days. If past observations can be weighted un-equally then more weight can be given to recent observations so that large jumps in volatility are not caused by events that happened a long time ago. However, this method still relies on the assumption that future volatilities are based on historic price movements.

It does avoid the pitfalls of the correlation (or covariance methods), ie, normally distributed returns, constant correlations and constant deltas. These are not then needed to calculate VaR by historical simulation. Historical volatility does capture the non-normal distribution of risk factor returns. Consequently allowance is made for one-off market events. It is, however, because of the weighting and the revaluing of the portfolio at different levels, more computationally intensive than the covariance method.

Monte Carlo simulation method

This is the most computer intensive method of the three VaR methodologies and also the most flexible. The risk manager will use historical distributions for risk factor returns. A large number of randomly-generated different simulations (say 10,000) are then run forward in time by using volatility and correlation estimates chosen by the risk manager. When all the simulations are done the VaR can be found by listing all the outcomes in order of profit and loss and cutting off at the required confidence level. The cutting off point represents the VaR.

Stress testing

Whichever method is used, stress testing - that is applying the equivalent of a major market movement, ie, Black Wednesday to the VaR methodology - will ensure that the overall market risk is within the limits of the capital requirements and can be absorbed by the financial institution.

Back testing

It is also necessary to look at past VaR reports and redefine them against what actually happened in the markets. This will ensure that the methodology employed by an institution is at the least accurate to within acceptable bounds.

Sine qua non conditions for successful risk management

The mechanical actions required from the back office to assist in risk management have been detailed in the first sections of this book. In the following pages, we look at the additional factors in this area which can increase/decrease the risks.

Investigation

Back office support check confirmations

The timely despatch of the host bank's confirmations and the checking of incoming broker and counterparties' confirmations can be a critical process in the settlements environment. This is especially true where formal SSI agreements do not exist between the banks (London Code of Conduct, p.13/14, s.88/89). It is at this stage that errors not identified at the initial capture can be spotted and corrected before the value date or maturity date of the trade.

Undetected errors can lead to monetary losses to one or both parties to the trade and it is therefore important that confirmations received are checked for accuracy as quickly as possible. The importance of accurately checking confirmations and providing the technology and level of staffing to adequately complete this task is essential if errors and subsequent penalty claims are to be kept to a minimum.

Prompt action in identifying and correcting errors can considerably reduce or even totally avoid monetary losses being incurred by one or both parties to the trade. Some internal rules should be in place that stipulate the maximum number of days that can elapse before a missing confirmation is followed up; under what circumstances matters should be referred to management, etc. Failure to adhere to these instructions could be momentous since failure to send confirmations has been the first indication that a bank is in trouble - especially when the trade would now be in a significant loss situation.

ACS

This acronym stands for automated confirmation system which, although initially created by a group of banks and brokers, now mostly feeds in direct to BART and TRAM as part of the overall solution to faster and more efficient matching of trades. It was founded in 1986 and now has 500 customers across 30 countries with offices in London, Hong Kong, New York, Singapore, Sydney and Toronto.

The system effectively short-cuts the delivery of paper-based confirmations which would need separate generation and physical delivery to the counterparty by providing automatic electronic messages from the broker to the bank as the details are entered at the broker's office.

The whole ACS, BART and TRAM system in the UK greatly assists in this context. The specific BART benefits are:

- Reduced risk of financial loss.
- Increased security.
- Improved processing efficiency.
- Time saved on investigations.

The specific benefits of TRAM are:

- Reduced settlement errors and related costs.
- Increased productivity.
- Faster matching.
- Greater staff motivation.
- Up-to-the-moment management information.

Record trading transactions accurately

The middle/back office

The increase in product types and the resulting surge in volumes have placed great strain on the back office. Technology development has absorbed pure volumes in relation to the increases in staffing levels, but risk is a key driver in the demand for processing systems development. Additionally, there are several factors affecting processing systems:

- Increasing volumes.
- Complex instruments.
- Need to reduce risk.
- Need to reduce cost.

These result in the simple fact that: Time = Risk = Cost. Risk varies according to currency and maturity (see Figure 8.2).

The solution that banks, technology vendors/developers, and Reuters and SWIFT are all focusing development on is straight through processing. As already mentioned in Chapter 2, straight through processing is the processing of trade data with the minimum of manual intervention, the complete removal of paper from the trading process. These are tickets, confirmation faxes/telexes or payment instructions. For this to become reality there are six principles to follow:

- Capture data at its source.
- Eliminate re-keying.
- Encourage vendor choice.
- Use modular components.
- Use open systems.
- Follow industry standards.

Those of us who have been operation managers over the years have our concerns. What is clear is that, without very stringent controls on the trader's desk that validates his authority to trade in the product with the counterparty and within his position limits, there could be a situation where a 'Nick Leeson' result could re-occur.

Theoretically automation will reduce this risk, but is likely to be implemented initially with the traditional and standard market products like FX spot. The more complex products will follow on, but then that is and always has been the way. You cannot have a system without the product, and 'rocket scientist' traders continue to create new types of products.

Providing timely information to management

Nostro reconciliation

What does management want to see in terms of reporting? Whilst there are many types of report, many based on the personal needs of the manager, the critical information/report management required is the nostro reconciliation (see also page 50). This is the reconciliation of payment in and out of the nostro accounts to the relative bank statements. The reconciliation will list all open items.

Figure 8.2 Risk profile.

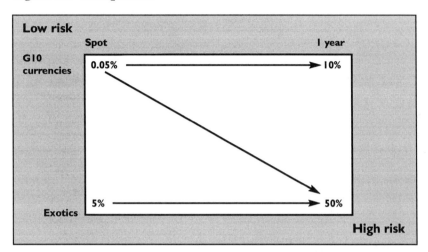

Most institutions will, at senior level, issue a directive that reconciliation of a nostro's suspense account is done promptly and in accordance with the accounting and operation manuals. Nostro reconciliation must be done daily, and open items acted upon immediately. It is far easier to resolve investigations if acted upon immediately. The longer an item is left unresolved, the harder it becomes to clear, and the penalty claim (risk) will be significantly higher.

Nostro reconciliation should be done by a person who is not involved in:

- Originating transactions.
- Responding to transactions.
- Authorising transactions.

The report should also contain the following:

- The difference or outstanding amount.
- The product or instrument.
- The trader and operational department.
- The cause of the difference or outstanding amount.

Any posting of penalty/loss should be accompanied by an error report, with a comment on what steps have been taken to rectify the causes. Most losses will be as a combination of:

- Computer/telecom fault.
- Procedural deficiency.
- Control failure.
- Unclear instructions.
- Human error.
- Other.

Reporting should include to the head of operations and the head of trading and possibly the general manager. The auditing department needs to be involved in the investigation. The cash management desk of a trading room should also be advised of any non receipts before the report is issued, as short cash positions may need to be covered promptly (market risk). Management will need to be aware of volumes of transactions and set performance targets (benchmarking) for the various steps in the transaction process. Improvements can be measured by the level of nostro outstandings in relation to the volume.

Audit support: internal and external staff

The role of the auditor has always been one of suspicion to the trader and his back office support groups. However an independent review of the transaction process is essential to controlling risk from inception to settlement of a transaction. Audit has a separate reporting line, usually directly to general management.

Copies of all significant reports will also be sent to audit. Here consolidation of market and counterparty risk will take place, and reconciliation to the general ledger of the bank undertaken. Audit reports are a regular feature of operations and trading life, with reporting copied to general management or board level.

External auditors provide a further check on the banks' processes, and provide important verification of the institutions annual accounts.

One increasing area of audit concern is the control of 24-hour trading. As the euro becomes established, this area could become of yet higher focus. Although it will be management that approves/forbids such trading and sets the paramaters, there will, of necessity, be a role for back office to provide separate and timely reports of all the deals contracted outside of their own centre's trading hours and confirmation that all controls have been properly monitored, input actioned at the appropriate time and the positions correctly adjusted before reports are sent to management. It may well also entail the maintenance and advice to other counterparties of the bank's policy and the names of the staff authorised to carry out such activities.

Daily mark to market

When a trader takes a position in a currency or bond or option, he will have paid a price for that instrument/currency. That position is then subject to changes in price through the normal supply and demand pressures created throughout the trading day. At the end of each trading day the close of business price is compared to the purchase price of the instrument. In this way unrealised profit or loss can be determined for the trading book.

External valuation

External auditors during the course of their annual review will review the basis upon which market risk is calculated. All annual reports must include a section on off balance sheet risk. It usually specifies the nominal value (NPV) of the forward and derivative positions and the replacement value.

Regulators such as the SFA and the Bank of England also will keep an eye on the exposures generated by trading activities. Each financial institution will have its own regulatory body to which it must report, on a regular basis, the trading exposure. The regulatory bodies may have their own methodology on how to calculate and report market risk but the BIS capital accord is designed to generate a consistent method that is accepted and implemented internationally.

Limits

We have talked about how we determine the VaR for different currencies, settlement risks and replacement risk for counterparties and how we report these exposures to management. We need now to talk about internal limits, how they are set and how we use them in excess reporting. Also it is important that each institution puts in place an effective disciplinary procedure for traders who exceed either counterparty or market limits. This should include, in the most blatant cases, dismissal.

The BIS recommendations adopted by banks by the end of 1997 (for the first time) include for capital purposes market risk. It can be argued therefore that market risk in addition to credit risk is now a cost to the bank. Therefore the setting and use of limits must be managed prudently.

Country limits

This category will include the following types of risk:

- Counterparty replacement risk relative to the country of incorporation for all traded instruments including derivatives.
- Currency risk, eg, the exposure in VaR for the country of the relative currency.
- The relative government bonds (issuer risk).
- Eurobonds issued by non-government institutions (issuer risk). (Yankee Bonds issued in the US domestic market by a foreign borrower. The issuer risk is with the country of the issuer.)
- Settlement risk (overnight).

Obviously the main western economies (G10) will probably be given an open limit with no constraints on total exposure at all. However careful monitoring of exposures to emerging markets or the weaker economies (eg, some African countries) is necessary and limits need to be realistic.

From time to time approved excessions occur for good business reasons. For example, if a trader sees an arbitrage opportunity between the Swedish government bond price and the gilt, he may wish to buy as much Swedish paper as possible, having firstly been given prior approval from the banker responsible for Sweden. Country limits will include all counterparty risk and, under the BIS Capital Accord, market risk originating from the respective country.

Currency limits

Most banks in the City of London trade in the main G10 currencies. Even though these countries have stable economies it is necessary to establish limits that are indicative of the amounts or exposure measured in terms of VaR a bank is prepared to risk for, say, holding periods of overnight, 10 days, a month, etc.

The limits are set by currency or desk. The FX spot desk, for example, will have overall limits for USD, CHF, EUR, etc. The fixed income traders will have limits based on the trading book, ie, euro sterling, US government bonds, etc, still based on currencies of the bonds rather that the issuer.

Systems need to be developed that can apply the VaR for each currency against the limit of the desk and on to the overall limit of the currency across all products on the trading floor. Real time systems, which remain rare (only used by large investment houses or clearers) must report excessions allowing accurate decisions to be made based on client orders or large currency movements that are traded on and off the relative desks or trading books.

Settlement exposure

Limits set for settlement are usually called daily settlement lines (DSLs). They reflect the total amount to be settled between counterparties on one business day. The limit applied will reflect the volume of business undertaken with a particular counterparty and include any bilateral or multilateral netting agreements in place.

The more sophisticated the system, the more accurate the limits. The limits can be multi product, after all settlement of cash is the same regardless of the product, however this assumes that settlements from many different systems can be amalgamated under one limit.

Duration of settlement exposure

Because we are measuring the total amount to be settled on one day with a single counterparty technically the line begins each day at zero and, assuming everything settles, finishes the day on zero. However confirmation of settlement from, say, the US will not be received until the next morning, yet another reason for prompt nostro reconciliation. This therefore can be redefined as overnight settlement exposure.

Another type of settlement exposure is called intraday settlement exposure. The payments are made in the morning and through the processing delay receipts are received in the afternoon. At around midday the intraday exposure can typically be at minus 3 billion dollars for a bank. Each bank has this same type of exposure although not quite on the same scale. Payments are made in the morning and receipts are received in the afternoon.

Stop loss/profit orders

The daily mark-to-market report will give a good indication of any specific position that is causing concern through an unrealised loss. A limit that sets the amount an institution is prepared to lose if markets move against you must be established. Some traders stick to a loss making position because they believe it will eventually make money. However, because the trading book is for short-term investments and management may not share the same view as the trader, procedures to close out the position when a certain limit is reached must be in place.

Another aspect is when trading institutions receive requests from customers, branches and correspondents to buy or sell a fixed amount of currency if the exchange rate for that currency reaches a specified level. This type of request which includes stop-loss and limit orders is growing, mainly because of the increasing sophistication of risk management techniques, supported by technology development. Management therefore needs to ensure that there is a clear understanding between its institution and its counterparties on the basis that these orders will be undertaken. In accepting such an order the institution can only agree to make every reasonable effort to execute the order quickly at the established price. Disputes can occur particularly at times of peak volume and extreme volatility and consequent investigations may be hard to prove one way or another.

The regulatory environment: BIS recommendations (1996)

The risk measurement framework

As from the end of 1997 banks were required to measure and apply capital charges in respect of their market risks in addition to their credit risks. Market risk is defined as the risk of losses in on and off balance sheet positions arising from movements in market prices. The precise risks subject to this agreement are:

- Risks pertaining to interest rate related instruments and equities in the trading book.
- Foreign exchange risk and commodities risk throughout the bank.

Scope and coverage of the capital charges

The capital charges for interest rate related instruments and equities will apply to the current market value of items in banks' trading books. The trading book includes proprietary positions held for short term resale and where profits/losses are expected from movements in the price. Positions from matched principal brokering and market making, or positions taken in order to hedge other elements of the trading book are also included in the capital charge.

The banking book may be hedged or include instruments that may be used as part of the trading book. The banking book which includes proprietary positions that are for long-term investment and their respective hedges are not to be included in the market risk capital charge. In practice these investments will fall under the credit risk capital charge. Most reputable institutions have a clear division between the market traders and those employees responsible for long-term investment. The committee will monitor the way in which banks allocate financial instruments between the trading and banking books. The capital charges for foreign exchange risk and for commodities risk will apply to the banks' total currency and commodity positions.

The capital requirements for market risk are to apply on a world-wide consolidated basis. Where appropriate national authorities may permit banking and financial entities in a group which is running a global consolidated book and whose capital is being assessed on a global basis, to report long and short options in the same instrument on a net basis no matter where they are booked. However, in certain circumstances supervisory authorities may demand that the individual positions be taken into the system without any offsetting or netting against the remainder of the group.

General market risk

The capital requirement for general market risk is designed to capture the risk of loss arising from changes in interest rates. A choice between two methods, *maturity* and *duration*, is allowed. In each method the capital charge is the sum of four components:

*   The net short or long position in the trading book.
*   A small proportion of the matched positions in each time band (the vertical disallowance).
*   A larger proportion of matched positions across different time bands (the horizontal disallowance).
*   A net charge for positions in options.

Separate maturity ladders should be used for each currency and capital charges calculated for each currency separately and summed with no offsetting between positions of the opposite sign.

The maturity method

In the maturity method long or short positions in debt securities and other sources of interest rate exposure, including derivatives, are slotted into a maturity ladder as shown in Table 8.2. Fixed rate instruments should be allocated according to the residual term to maturity and floating rate instruments according to the residual term to the next repricing date. Opposite positions of the same amount and maturity can be omitted.

Table 8.2   Time bands and weights.

Coupon 3% or more	Coupon less than 3%	Risk weight	Assumed changes in yield
1 mth or less	1 mth or less	0.00%	1.00
1 to 3 mths	1 to 3 mths	0.20%	1.00
3 to 6 mths	3 to 6 mths	0.40%	1.00
6 to 12 mths	6 to 12 mths	0.70%	1.00
1 to 2 yrs	1.0 to 1.9 yrs	1.25%	0.90
2 to 3 yrs	1.9 to 2.8 yrs	1.75%	0.80
3 to 4 yrs	2.8 to 3.6 yrs	2.25%	0.75
4 to 5 yrs	3.6 to 4.3 yrs	2.75%	0.75
5 to 7 yrs	4.3 to 5.7 yrs	3.25%	0.70
7 to 10 yrs	5.7 to 7.3 yrs	3.75%	0.65
10 to 15 yrs	7.3 to 9.3 yrs	4.50%	0.60
15 to 20 yrs	9.3 to 10.6 yrs	5.25%	0.60
Over 20 yrs	10.6 to 12 yrs	6.00%	0.60
	12 to 20 yrs	8.00%	0.60
	Over 20 yrs	12.50%	0.60

The first step is to weight the positions in each time band by the factor designed to reflect the price sensitivity of those positions to assumed changes in interest rates. The second step is to offset the weighted longs and shorts in each time band, resulting in a single short or long position for each band. A 10% capital charge will be levied on the smaller of the offsetting positions to reflect basis and gap risk, as the positions include different instruments and maturities, eg:

The weighted long position is $100 m.
The weighted short position is $90 m.

Table 8.3 Horizontal disallowances.

Zones	Time band	Within the zone	Between adjacent zones	Between zones 1 and 3
Zone 1	0 to 1 mth	40%		
	1 to 3 mths			
	3 to 6 mths			
	6 to 12 mths		40%	
Zone 2	1 to 2 years	30%		
	2 to 3 years			
	3 to 4 years			100%
Zone 3	4 to 5 years		40%	
	5 to 7 years			
	7 to 10 years	30%		
	10 to 15 years			
	15 to 20 years			
	Over 20 years			

The so called *vertical disallowance* for that time band is 10% of $90m or $9 million.

This calculation produces two sets of weighted positions. The net long or short position in each time band ($10m in the above example) and the vertical disallowance.

In addition banks will be allowed to conduct two rounds of horizontal off-setting. Firstly between the net position in the three different time bands (0 to 1 year, 1 to 4 years and 4 years and over) and subsequently between the net positions in the three different time bands. The offsetting will be subject to a scale of disallowances expressed as a fraction of the matched positions (see Table 8.3). The weighted long and short positions in each of the three zones may be offset, subject to the matched portion attracting a disallowance factor that is part of the capital charge. The residual net position in each zone may be carried over and offset against opposite positions in other zones to a second set of disallowance factors.

The duration method

This is a more accurate method of measuring general risk in which banks measure all their general market risk by calculating the price sensitivity of each position separately. This requires supervisory consent and will be subject to supervisory monitoring of the systems used to calculate the sensitivity.

The mechanics of this method are as follows:

* First calculate the price sensitivity of each instrument in terms of an interest rate change in interest rates of between 0.6 and 1.0 percentage points depending on the maturity of the instrument.
* Slot the resulting sensitivity measure into the duration-based ladder (see Table 8.4).
* Subject long and short positions in each time band to a 5% vertical disallowance designed to capture basis risk.
* Carry forward the net positions in each time bands for horizontal offsetting subject to the disallowances set out in the horizontal disallowance (see Table 8.3).

Interest rate derivatives

Interest rate derivatives are FRAs, bond futures, interest rate and cross currency swaps and forward FX positions. They should also be converted into positions in the relevant underlying and become subject to the charges as described in Table 8.5. The amounts reported should be the market value of the principal amount of the underlying or of the notional underlying.

Futures and FRAs are treated as a combination of a long and a short position in a notional government security. The maturity of a future or FRA will be the period until delivery or exercise of the contract plus, where applicable, the life of the underlying instrument. For example, a long position in a June three-month interest rate future taken in April is to be reported as a long position in a government security with a maturity of five months and a short position in a government security with a maturity of two months.

Swaps are treated as two notional positions in government securities with relevant maturities. If a bank is receiving floating and paying fixed, this is seen as a long position in an instrument with a maturity at the next repricing date and a short position in a fixed rate instrument with the maturity of the residual life of the swap.

Table 8.4   Duration method: time bands and assumed changes in yield.

Zones	Time band	Assumed change in yield
Zone 1	1 mth or less	1.00
	1 to 3 mths	1.00
	3 to 6 mths	1.00
	6 to 12 mths	1.00
Zone 2	1.0 to 1.9 yrs	0.90
	1.9 to 2.8 yrs	0.80
	2.8 to 3.6 yrs	0.75
Zone 3	3.6 to 4.3 yrs	0.75
	4.3 to 5.7 yrs	0.70
	5.7 to 7.3 yrs	0.65
	7.3 to 9.3 yrs	0.60
	9.3 to 10.6 yrs	0.60
	10.6 to 12 yrs	0.60
	12 to 20 yrs	0.60
	Over 20 yrs	0.60

Calculation of capital charges under the standardised methodology

Allowable offsets

Excluded from the calculation are long and short positions in identical instruments with exactly the same issue, coupon, currency and maturity. Also excluded is a matched position in a future or forward and its corresponding underlying. There is no offsetting in positions in different currencies: the separate legs of a cross currency swap or FX forwards are to be treated as notional positions in the relevant instruments and included in the calculation for each currency.

Table 8.5   Summary of treatment of interest rate derivatives

Instrument	Specific risk charge	General market risk charge
Exchange traded future		
Government debt security	No	Yes, as two positions
Corporate debt security	Yes	Yes, as two positions
Index on interest rates	No	Yes, as two positions
OTC forward		
Government debt security	No	Yes, as two positions
Corporate debt security	Yes	Yes, as two positions
Index on interest rates	No	Yes, as two positions
FRAs/swaps	No	Yes, as two positions
Forward foreign exchange	No	Yes, as one position in each currency

Additionally, offsets in certain conditions are allowed in the following cases:

•   The underlying must be of the same nominal value and denominated in the same currency.

•   For futures: the products must be identical and mature within seven days of each other.

•   For swaps and FRAs: the reference rate (for floating rate positions) must be identical and the coupon closely matched (within 15 basis points).

•   For swaps, FRAs and forwards: the next interest fixing day, or for fixed coupon positions or forwards, the residual maturity must correspond within the following limits:
     Less than one month, hence same day.
     Between one month and one year, hence within seven days.
     Over one year, hence within 30 days.

Flexibility in approach is allowed if approved by the supervisory authority (see Table 8.5) and regularly monitored. For example, institutions with large swap books may wish to convert the payments into present value and a single net figure entered into the appropriate time band using procedures that apply to zero or low coupon bonds.

Interest rate and currency swaps, FRAs, forward FX contracts and interest rate futures on an interest rate index (eg, LIBOR) will not be subject to a specific risk charge (eg, credit).

Once again, the responsibility upon the back office would be to advise management of any changes in pattern of trade with such entries and/or confirmation/settlement problems.

Total global FX turnover was estimated at $1,260 billion in April 1998 net of double counting with the gross at $1,490 billion ($1,190 billion in 1995) (see Table 8.6).

Significantly, although there had been growth in the FX markets, the major changes were reflected in the derivatives markets - although the total for emerging markets was only $12.5 billion. Somewhat unexpectedly, London was the main gainer being over twice the size of its nearest rival - the US. Whilst London's FX growth was lower than the comparative US figure, London was still 82% higher than New York - the next biggest.

One other feature was that the share of 'other financial institutions' was up from 9% to 24%. This would be the share of pension funds, hedge funds and building societies.

The capital requirements

Bank for International Settlements (BIS)

The BIS is the central banks' central bank which in 1987 brought out new capital adequacy requirements based on a basic 8% rule. This led to the Basle Agreement of 1987 for implementation by 1993 latest. In this the minimum targets set were:

- Capital: risk-assets of 8%.
- Core capital: total capital base of 50%.
- Core capital: total assets of 4%.

Table 8.6   BIS three-yearly survey of market turnover (source: Bank of England).

Average daily FX turnover		
Country	**April 1998 ($bn)**	**Percentage growth over 1995**
UK	637	37
US	350	43
Japan	149	-8
Singapore	139	32
Germany	94	24
Switzerland	82	-5
Hong Kong	79	-13
France	72	24
OTC derivative average daily turnover		
Country	**April 1998 ($bn)**	**Percentage growth over 1995**
UK	171	131
US	91	75
France	46	107
Japan	42	-28
Germany	34	162
Switzerland	16	256
Singapore	11	-38
Hong Kong	4	-11

Each category of asset was given a weighting to arrive at a 'risk-assets' figure, for example:

- Domestic government: Nil.
- Cash: Nil.
- Claims on other OECD banks: 20%.
- Mortgage loans to owner-occupiers: 50%.
- Other claims on the non-bank private sector: 100%.
- Claims on non-OECD banks: 100%.
- Aggregate net short open FX positions: 100%.

Similarly each type of off-balance sheet instrument was given a weighting. This was set at 8% of the default risk - effectively 8% of any contract that is in profit - when marked-to-market. However, all off-balance sheet (OBS) instruments carry far lower weightings and thus permit considerable leverage and hedging potential.

Since the initial capital adequacy requirements were introduced, some refinements have been put in place via the Capital Adequacy Directive (CAD) of 1993 which extended minimum capital requirements upon all credit institutions and investment firms in respect of market risk and other risks associated with the trading book, ie, beyond counterparty risk and instrument risk. CAD introduced the differentiation between a banking book and a trading book with a distinction between the two's risk profile.

At the same time a new tier of capital was introduced - Tier 3 equals up to two years subordinated debt and daily net trading profits, to be used principally to support the trading book. This change was made to allow the use of more flexible forms of capital to support risks arising from the trading book. To do this, the whole risk on the trading book as a whole will be assessed value at risk (VaR) instead of assessing each component part. This new approach would normally reduce the total value of risk-weighted assets and thus the capital required. As a result, the Basle Committee confirmed in 1996 the new approach to regulation in that:

- Market risk will be formally considered for supervisory purposes.
- A concession is now made to the commercial banks to use their own VaR models although they will be required to meet specific qualitative and quantitative criteria.

Division of risks

Each financial institution must now divide its balance sheet into a *banking* book and a *trading* book. Effectively this means that the 'normal' business of a bank is included in the 'banking' book with all the short-term speculative business in the 'trading' book. Thus the trading book contains:

* Transferable securities and units in collective investments.
* Money market instruments, not deposits and loans.
* Financial futures contracts, including cash settled instruments.
* FRAs.
* Interest rate, currency and equity swaps.
* Options on all of the above, especially on currency and interest rates.

The banking book still needs capital but as specified under original Basle 8% rules. The trading book is covering more than just counterparty risk and has to have its own rules and this has led to the creation of an additional tier of capital - Tier 3. Capital is thus now considered under:

Tier 1 - *Core capital*
>Permanent shareholders' equity.
>Allotted, called and fully paid-up preferred stock.
>Disclosed reserves.
>Interim declared profits (audited).
>Minority interests.

Tier 2 - *Supplementary capital*
>Reserves resulting from revalued fixed assets.
>General provisions.
>Hybrid capital - perpetual cumulative preferred
>shares and perpetual subordinated debt.
>Subordinated term debt.

Tier 3 - *Trading book ancillary capital*
>Short-term subordinated debt, minimum two years' original.
>Daily net trading book profits.

Total of Tier 2 cannot exceed 50% of Tier 1. Tier 2 capital used to meet banking book cannot exceed 100% of Tier 1 used for same purpose. Tier 2 and Tier 3 used to meet trading book capital must not in total exceed 200% of the Tier 1 capital used for same purpose. Total of Tier 2 and Tier 3 cannot normally exceed Tier 1.

The treatment of foreign currencies

Two processes are needed to calculate the capital requirement for foreign exchange risk:

- Measure the exposure in a single currency position.
- Measure the risks inherent in a bank's mix of long and short positions.

Measuring the exposure in a single currency

The banks' net open position in each currency should be calculated by summing:

- The net spot position (assets less liabilities, including accrued interest in the currency in question).
- The net forward position (including currency futures and principals on currency swaps not included in the spot position).
- Guarantees that are certain to be called and are likely to be irrecoverable.
- Net future income/expenses not yet accrued but already fully hedged.
- Any other item representing a profit or loss in foreign currencies.
- The net delta-based equivalent of the total book of foreign currency options.

Composite currencies such as the ECU could, until January 1999, be either reported as a separate currency or split into their component parts. Interest accrued should be included as a position. Accrued expenses should also be included.

Forward currency positions will be valued at the current spot rate. However, if banks value their positions using NPV then it is expected that this is the value to be included for the capital charge. No capital charge need apply to positions related to items that are deducted from a bank's capital base such as investments in a non consolidated subsidiary.

Measuring the FX risk in a portfolio of foreign currency positions

Banks may either use a method described in Table 8.7 which treats all currencies equally, or use an internal model that calculates the degree of risk dependant on the composition of the bank's portfolio.

Table 8.7   Calculation of capital requirement from FX position.

Yen	DEM	GBP	FFR	US$	Gold
+50	+100	+150	-20	-180	-35
+300			-200		35

The NPV of each currency is converted at spot rates into the reporting currency. The overall net position is measured by aggregating the sum of the net short positions or the sum of the net long positions, whichever is the greater, plus the net position (short or long) in gold (if traded). The capital charge would be 8% of the higher of either the net long currency positions or the net short currency positions (ie, 300) and the net position in gold (35) = 335 x 8% = 26.8.

SELF TESTS

1   The general management has announced that settlements and the FX trading desk will have to co-locate next to each other on the same floor as part of a cost-saving exercise. You are responsible for control within settlements. Outline your concerns and the measures that you would take to resolve them.

2   Describe the FX confirmation process, covering the reasons for sending confirmations, the advantages and disadvantages of the different methods of confirming and the control framework surrounding confirmations.

3   Describe briefly each of the following three topics:
a   Netting.
b   Nostro reconciliations.
c   Collateral.

4   Explain FX settlement risk and briefly outline the initiatives being taken to reduce this risk.

5   Explain real time gross settlement and briefly outline its benefits.

6   What are delivery versus payment (DVP) and payment versus payment (PVP) and their benefits?

7   Describe the advantages of SSIs when compared with deal by deal exchange of instructions.

8 What are the benefits of using the central money office (CMO) to deliver sterling securities?

Answers

1 The overriding concern relates to the segregation of duties between operations personnel and sales and trading personnel. Put very simply, this means there should be a clear split between the duties of the two functions, ie, the front office should enter into transactions, the back office should confirm and settle those transactions. Each should not undertake the other's functions. Without this basic segregation the risk of fraud arises as has been evidenced recently at both Barings PLC and Daiwa Bank.

Whilst it is always preferable to have distinct physical separation, eg, different buildings, floors or offices, a lack of such segregation may be acceptable, provided that it can be demonstrated that appropriate management controls (shown below) are in place. In any case, some basic separation, eg, screens, cupboards, etc, should be used wherever possible.

Operations personnel, who are responsible for confirmation and settlement, must maintain a reporting line independent of sales and trading, where the trade execution takes place.

Basic 'segregation' controls should be in place, for example, computer logical access controls. These ensure that front office personnel cannot access settlements systems and back office personnel cannot access deal capture systems (or relevant functionality contained therein).

Confirmations should be sent directly to, and from, back office staff.

The proximity of the two functions makes it all the more important to ensure that the segregation of duties is maintained at all times.

2 A confirmation is the record of the terms of the transaction that should be sent out by each party, within one to three hours of trade time. The confirmation provides a necessary *final* check against dealing errors and should be independent of the trading room and be performed entirely by operations. Using data from the settlements and payments systems the confirmations provide a check to ensure that the operations areas of each institution have recorded the same details for each transaction. For this reason, Reuter deal checks and trader call backs do not constitute a substitute for proper confirmations.

The confirmation should contain (at a minimum) counterparties and location, broker (where appropriate), transaction date, value date, currency amounts (bought and sold), exchange rate and settlement instructions.

The most common forms of confirmation, from least preferable to most preferable, are by phone, mail, fax, telex, SWIFT. The electronic forms of transmission are preferable as they are faster. Of these, the use of the fax requires extra diligence because of the risks involved, ie, fax is not a secure method.

Operations is responsible for checking inbound confirmations carefully upon receipt and for monitoring all unconfirmed transactions. Risk in the confirmation process arises either when discrepancies are missed or when trades are not confirmed. Standard escalation procedures should be in place to pursue and resolve discrepancies.

3a There are two types of netting, payment netting and close-out (credit) netting. Payment netting is the practice of combining all trades between two counterparties and calculating a single net payment in each currency for each value date. It may be conducted on a bilateral or multilateral basis. The establishment of payment netting between counterparties is useful in reducing settlement risk, operational risk and operational costs. FX Net is an example of a bi-lateral payment netting system.

Close-out netting relates to the final settlement of any unsettled contracts in the event of a counterparty default. This would result in a single net obligation (from the closing-out and netting of all unrealised gains and losses) that is either payable or receivable, thus removing the possibility of 'cherry-picking'. The operational process of payment netting should be supported by a legal agreement and legal opinions confirming enforceability in relevant jurisdictions. This agreement usually takes the form of a multi-page master agreement incorporating close-out netting. ECHO is a clearing house that supports multilateral payment and close-out netting.

b The nostro reconciliation occurs at the end of the trade settlement process to ensure a trade has settled properly and that all the expected cash flows have occurred. This involves a comparison of expected cash movements and actual cash movements both paid out and received by the nostro bank. The reconciliation should take place as soon as possible on value date and in no instance should it be done later than the day following settlement date. The process should be automated wherever possible. If any differences occur the operations must follow-up with sales & trading and/or the counterparty to resolve the discrepancy. The cause of the discrepancy might be that wrong settlement or trade information was captured, or that the nostro bank made an error. In the event of late payment the culpable party would then arrange to pay with good value or pay compensation.

c   Collateral is an asset pledged to a counterparty, who in turn has the right to apply it against any losses that the counterparty may incur if the counterparty pledging the asset defaults. Collateralized trading is known as margin trading in certain markets. Typically a collateral taker would require an initial margin and subsequent variation margin dependant upon the daily mark-to-market on both the collateral and the trading position supported. Use of collateralised trading may reduce credit (replacement and settlement) risk but it does not eliminate the need for a credit decision. This will be required for the type and amount of collateral required for each counterparty. Similarly there are both legal (related to good title to the assets) and operational risks associated with (the taking of collateral) that have to be addressed. Collateralised trading has opened up various markets to smaller investors and asset/investment managers who may previously not have had such access owing to credit considerations.

Examples of commonly used collateralized trading facilities are: Repo futures (margin) and FX.

4   FX settlement risk is the risk that one party to an FX trade delivers the sold currency to the counterparty but does not receive the purchased currency from the counterparty.

The reduction of FX settlement risk is being actively pursued by the regulatory authorities following the publication, in March 1996, by the Bank for International Settlements of the report prepared by the Committee on Payment and Settlement Systems of the central banks of the Group of Ten countries. The initiatives being taken are:

• Adoption of the best practice recommendations for measuring and managing FX settlement exposures.
• Use of well-founded bilateral or multilateral netting schemes, such as FX Net and ECHO.
• The enhancement of national payment systems to incorporate real time gross settlement (RTGS).
• The project set up by the 'Group of 20' banks to explore the feasibility of establishing a multi-currency settlement service to achieve PVP for FX settlements.

5 RTGS is the real time settlement of payments in central bank funds by means of direct postings to the settlement accounts of each of the settlement banks. The benefits are:
- The receipt of guaranteed funds and finality of settlement
- The reduction in the possibility of the incidence of systemic risk.
- This provides the foundation stone for the implementation of DVP for securities settlements and PVP for FX settlements.

6 DVP is the simultaneous exchange of payment against the delivery of securities whereby good title passes against the receipt of guaranteed funds.

The benefits are:
- It eliminates the risk that one party to the transaction may default to the disadvantage of the other party, who has or will settle their side of the transaction, ie, if payment is made then the securities will be received and vice versa.

- PVP is the simultaneous exchange of the two payments of an FX transaction with the delivery and receipt of guaranteed funds.

The main benefit is:
- It eliminates the risk that one party to the transaction may default to the disadvantage of the other party, who has or will settle their side of the transaction, ie, if payment of the sold currency is made then the purchased currency will be received.

7 The main advantages are:
- *Security:* By exchanging standard settlement instructions which are confirmed by authenticated SWIFT message, tested telex or letter bearing two verified authorised signatures, the risk of fraud is virtually eliminated.
- *Settlement risk:* Where instructions are exchanged on a deal by deal basis, either by the traders or in the back offices, there is a risk of misunderstanding or misinterpretation of information as well as of transposition errors when keying the information into systems. These errors can result in serious financial losses in the form of overdraft interest claims as well as damage to relationships between counterparties when responsibility for such errors is disputed.
- *Processing efficiency:* The use of SSIs provides the following savings/benefits:
  Reduces time/effort of deal input.

Eliminates requirement for back-office to swap instructions over the telephone.

Reduces level of confirmation discrepancies and the associated time/effort in resolving them.

Enables greater level of automation thereby reducing staff costs and exchange risk. (By speeding up the process of exchanging confirmations, errors may be detected and corrected earlier.)

8 During the boom of the 1980s it was decided that the increasing number of physical sterling negotiable paper being walked around the city was unacceptable. The Bank of England introduced a system whereby paper can be transferred through a system by book entry transfer, the Central Moneymarkets Office (CMO) service.

Members of the service can now deliver large amounts of paper around the city within minutes in electronic form, rather than physically issuing the paper, getting each individual piece signed (normally twice), then requesting a member of staff (usually a messenger) to walk the paper, sometimes miles away, to the correct buyer.

The payments are automated. The seller enters a consideration amount which, on completion of the trade by the buyer, debits the buyer's account and credits the seller's account, thus saving costs by eliminating the need for bankers' payments, cheques, etc, and making the payment process quicker and more secure.

The delivery through CMO also decreases the chances of fraud and theft by restricting deliveries to members of the service and eliminating the movement and storage of the physical paper.

With physical paper the buyer has to check all signatures and store the paper, thus slowing the process and causing the buyer to equip the office with strong rooms or safes. With CMO the paper is managed at the B of E, thus these problems are avoided.

To sum up CMO is:

* Quicker: Physical deliveries are governed by people being available to walk perhaps several miles.
* Safer: Walking large numbers of CDs around London can be dangerous and open to theft or loss.
* More secure: Physical paper has to be stored in large safes, whereas non physical paper is held at the B of E.

CASE STUDIES

Case study 1

You receive your SWIFT statement from your USD correspondent, Citibank, New York, showing the following entries:

DEBITS

Amount	Ref	Value date
5,000,000.00	AIBLGB2L	961016
7,500,000.00	MIDIUS3 3	961015
9,247,500.00	OELBATWW	961016
10,000,000.00	MGTCFFPP	961016

CREDITS

Amount	Ref	Value date
1,001,447.50	CRLYGB2L	961016
8,567,600.00	DEUTDBFF	961016
10,000,000.00	RBCFXDEPTTOR	961016
25,000,000.00	BANK TOKYO	961016

Your *general ledger* for Citibank, New York, shows:

DEBITS

Amount	Ref	Value date
8,567,600.00	DEUTDEFF	961016
10,000,000.00	ROYLCATT	961016
10,014,475.00	CRLYGB2L	961016
25,000,000.00	BOFTJPJT	961016

CREDITS

Amount	Ref	Value date
5,000,000.00	ALLIEDIMSHLDN	961016
7,500,000.00	MIDIUS3 3	961016
9,247,500.00	OSTLAND WIEN	961016
10,000,000.00	MGTCFFPP	961016

1 How would you reconcile the above entries?
2 How would you resolve any discrepancies?

Case study 2

As the brokerage clerk, upon reconciling ABC Brokers' monthly account, you discover that two trades which should have been net of brokerage have actually been included and charged on the invoice for a total of £847.50.

The monthly bill, *after* the application of a 30% discount, is for £10,470.60. Assuming that both deals are subsequently agreed as being net of brokerage, recalculate the amount of commission due to the broker.

Case study 3

A SWIFT MT202 payment order in respect of a JPY loan to Barclays Bank, London, has been sent to your nostro correspondent bank, Sumitomo, Tokyo, with the wrong value date, ie, value 17/10/96 when it should have been value 18/10/96.

It is now 17.00 hours on 17/10/96. What would be the best way to rectify the situation?

Case study 4

It is 17.00 hours. You, the reconciliations clerk, are the only person left in the back office. The late shift dealer upon checking the Reuters 2001 hard copy of deals concluded today discovers that there is a USD/JPY deal ticket that has not been written out for value tomorrow.

The deal is our sale of 5 yards of JPY (5,000,000,000). What could you do?

Case study 5

It is 15.20 hours when your MM dealers discover they are still £5,000,000 short. They can only cover their shortage by effecting a GBP/USD overnight swap (buy GBP, sell USD value today; sell GBP buy USD value tomorrow) with a London bank.

Assuming this course of action is agreed and taken, what action is necessary by the back office?

Case study 6

You are the confirmations clerk and have received a confirmation from BCI Milan re their purchase of JPY 10 yards value tomorrow. They have confirmed payment to Bank of Tokyo, Tokyo, but your SSI data base says 'Sumitomo, Tokyo'. What action should you take?

Answers

Case study 1

1 You would mark off all ledger CRs and DRs that match *exactly* (in amount, beneficiary and value date) with the statement DRs and CRs.

2 To resolve the discrepancies - namely an apparent debit a day early for the USD 7,500,000 and the wrong statement CR of only USD 10,000,000 compared with your expected ledger DR of 10,014,750 - you would first need to obtain your original SWIFT messages to ensure they tally with the deal tickets. If they do not tally, then you would have to send amendments to Citibank.

Assuming they do tally, then you would need to contact Citibank to enquire why the USD 7,500,000 was debited a day early (and pre-advise them that you may need to claim for O/D charges if they cannot correct with good value).

For the shortfall on the CRLYGB2L deal, either Citibank have under-credited the account or Crédit Lyonnais, London, has sent the wrong instruction. (This could have been a deposit deal rolled over with interest and they have made it principal only.)

Case study 2

£10,470.60 x $\frac{100}{70}$ =£14,958.00 - 847.50 = £14,110.50 x 70% = £9,877.35

Case study 3

Ideally, if Barclays Bank, London, maintains its nostro at Sumitomo also, then you could try to instruct the nostro bank to adjust the value (MT999 would suffice) in your own and the beneficiary's account from 17/10 to 18/10. However, they may say they need to contact Barclays first.

However, if Barclays Bank, London, held its JPY account elsewhere, then you will need to ask BARCGB2L for one day's use of funds to mitigate your debit interest incurred at Sumitomo, Tokyo.

Case study 4

Attempt to locate someone in your New York office (because of the time difference) who has the authority to execute the payment order on your behalf. Also, the dealer may need reminding that he may have a deal to cover (with accompanying risk) based on the movement in rates against the rate on deal now discovered. Dealers should also be reminded to do the deal check earlier. (As clerk, you should ensure the incident is reported to the head of the back office).

Case study 5

Ensure receipt of the £5 million by CHAPS before 3.30 pm or via Bank of England after 3.30 pm and before 4.30 pm. Ensure payment of the USD by MT202 value today. Check the sterling dealer has advised the USD dealer of change to his/her position.

Case study 6

Check the actual confirmation. Based on what the confirmation says, refer the matter up and suggest pay according to the SSI received. Check with the SSI clerk to ascertain if there are any amended SSI instructions received recently from BCI. If time allows, revert direct to the counterparty to clarify situation. Send SWIFT to advise what you have done whether you have clarified the situation or not - MT399.

APPENDICES

APPENDIX 1

MARKET INTERACTIVITY

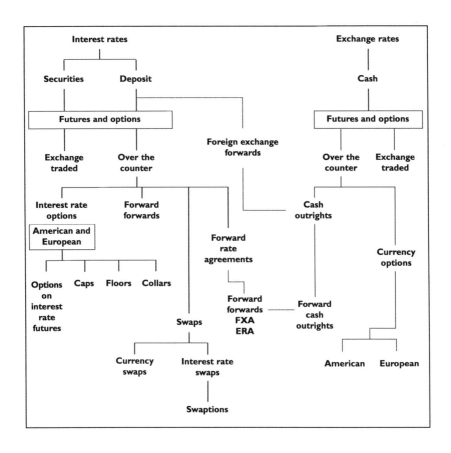

APPENDIX 2

MARKET AUTHORITIES/ DOCUMENTATION

IFEMA   International Foreign Exchange Master Agreement - governs all FX deals up to two years.

ICOM   International Currency Options Market - governs all option trades.

ISDA   International Swap and Derivative Association - international swap dealers' association swap documentation.

ISMA/PMA   International Securities and Market Association/Public Marketing Association - joint authorities governing repurchase business.

FRABBA   Forward Rate Agreement, British Bankers' Association - FRA standard documentation.

Appendix 3

Automated systems

Society for worldwide interbank financial telecommunications (SWIFT)

Some SWIFT message types are:

MT000-099	System messages.
MT100-199	Customer transfers, cheques.
MT200-299	Financial institution transfers.
MT300-399	FX, FX options, loans, deposits, FRAs, interest rate swaps.
MT400-499	Collections, cash letters.
MT500-599	Securities.
MT600-699	Precious metals syndications.
MT 700-799	Documentary credits, guarantees.
MT800-899	Traveller's cheques.
MT900-999	Balance reporting, rate changes, nostro statements, bilateral key exchange, netting, status enquiry.

Automated confirmation system (ACS)

This is the system into which brokers send deal details. Banks Automated Confirmation Reception Terminal (BART) is the banks' software equivalent and then Transaction Automatic Matching (TRAM) matches up what the brokers send and the banks have to find any exceptions. Major users of these facilities thus avoid the need to actually send 'paper' confirmations to their counterparties.

BART

BART is a PC based system, established in 1986, which provides a single point of control for your transactions. The main features are:

- Full audit controls - In-built audit facilities ensure that all received messages are automatically logged with date, time-stamp and sequence number to help you keep track of all transactions received and processed.
- Fast access to information - You can gain instant access to received data, whether for enquiry purposes, sorting or printing. Archive material can be retrieved within seconds and management reports automatically generated and distributed to other departments.
- Integrated treasury support - Automatic and seamless interfaces can link BART to your other systems such as those providing payment control, confirmation matching and brokerage management, thereby ensuring maximum benefit from the system.

The specific BART benefits are:

- Reduced risk of financial loss.
- Increased security.
- Improved processing efficiency.
- Time saved on investigations.

TRAM

This system can handle confirmations for foreign exchange or money market transactions, including CDs, FRAs and FX options, and can carry out the matching process against the details held in your in-house system against counterparty, broker or corporate confirmations whether received via SWIFT, ACS, Reuters or EBS and is thus 'real-time' - confirmations received by mail or telex are allowed for with only minimal entries required.

The system classifies the degree of matching as follows:

- *Paired* - all details match.
- *Proposed pair* - most details match but a visual check is required to allow/disallow the match.
- *Close fit* - confirmations differ in one or more of the mandatory fields (rate, amount, value date).
- *Time out* - here TRAM has not been able to find a match within a specified time limit and it needs to be investigated.

Management information is available initially in the form of a status screen which summarises the number of confirmations received from each source and their current matching status. Also other reports can be optionally obtained to highlight increases/decreases in volume for a particular type, differences in matching rates between types, etc. The following other specific optional modules are available:

- *Feedback:* This module ensures the status of deals, matched or otherwise, and is updated in the bank's in-house system, thereby ensuring that payments are not released until matching is perfect.
- *Chaser letters/SWIFT chasers:* According to a bank's own definition of overdue, the system can produce a chaser letter which, where SWIFT chaser letter is implemented, will then be automatically sent out via SWIFT.
- *Automated time out management system (ATOM):* This enhancement automatically sets and updates the time out values per counterparty. This then affords proactive management of potential losses should late confirmations be received.

The specific benefits of TRAM are:

- Reduced settlement errors and related costs.
- Increased productivity.
- Faster matching.
- Greater staff motivation.
- Up-to-the-moment management information.

Clearing house automated payments system (CHAPS)

This is a UK clearing system for large credit transfers. It has 14 member banks including the Bank of England. It settles on a multilateral basis at the end of each day and accounts for 92% of the value of total transactions.

Clearing house interbank payments system (CHIPS)

This is owned by the New York Clearing House Association. It settles payments multilaterally at the end of the day and has 122 participating banks (Edge Act banks, investment companies and commercial banks.)

Appendix 4

Settlement of transactions in the international securities market

Euroclear and Cedel are the two major depositories and settlement organisations in the international securities market. However, both institutions also accept and settle transactions involving domestic securities. Their combined turnover in 1992 amounted to US$ 14.5 trillion, or roughly US$ 55 billion on average per business day. Cedel was established in 1970. It handles 38 currencies, 33 markets and 80 countries. Its US$ turnover is 100 billion per day. Currently there is no bridge between Cedel and Euroclear. Euroclear was established in 1968. It handles over 100,000 different securities in 30 markets (mostly domestic) in 35 currencies. Its turnover in all currencies for the third quarter of 1998 was a total of the USD equivalent of 12.45 trillion, which equated to approximately USD 4.7 trillion per month or 200 billion per day.

The international securities market

The international securities market consists of a number of segments which have their own characteristics. They include the international bond market for long-term debt instruments (Euro-bonds and foreign bonds)* and the Euro-note market, where short-term paper such as commercial securities market is a multi-currency market; by far the largest proportion of

---

* Foreign bonds are issued in domestic capital markets by non-resident borrowers and underwritten and sold by a syndicate composed of institutions located in the country in which the bonds are offered (which may, however, include subsidiaries of multinational financial institutions). Euro-bonds are usually issued simultaneously in several capital markets and underwritten by an international syndicate (they are almost wholly exempt from disclosure and registration requirements and from withholding taxes). However, the distinction between Euro-bonds and foreign bonds has become increasingly blurred.

the stock of international bonds is denominated in US dollars (US$ 680 billion in 1992) with other currencies trailing well behind.

Since, in many countries, institutional investors are prohibited from buying unlisted securities, most international bonds are listed on established stock exchanges to improve their marketability. This is done, most commonly, on the Luxembourg Stock Exchange and the London Stock Exchange. Trading, however, is normally done over-the-counter and conducted by various specialised dealer groups. One particular feature of the international securities market is that most of the securities (especially in the Euro-markets) are in bearer form and are not fully dematerialised. In principle, the transfer of ownership can then take place through book entry in these security accounts. Furthermore, by simultaneously holding cash deposits with Euroclear and Cedel, users can also let the cash leg of the securities transactions be settled by these organisations. As a result, Euroclear and Cedel can be defined as both securities and large-value funds transfer systems.

Institutional characteristics

The Euroclear system is operated by Morgan Guaranty, Brussels, through a separate administrative unit called the Euroclear Operations Centre, under an operating agreement with the Euroclear Clearance System, *Société Coopérative,* set up under Belgian law. The Coopérative, in turn, is controlled partly by a large number of participants in the system (11.5% of its share capital) and by the UK-based Euroclear Clearance System Public Limited Company (88.5%). The latter company, which actually owns the system, is owned by 124 banks, brokers and investment institutions. Centrale de Livraison de Valeurs Mobilières (Cedel), société anonyme (SA) is a Luxembourg-based limited company which provides, in return for payment, for the circulation, custody and management of securities (and precious metals). It is currently owned by 108 shareholding financial institutions from some 20 different companies. Both institutions have customers or participants comprising major banks or security companies (about 2,500 each) in a large number of companies.* Reflecting the 'cooperative approach' taken by the owners of both the Euroclear and Cedel systems, no institution is entitled to hold more than a small fraction (3.25% and 5% respectively) of the shares in these companies.

Euroclear and Cedel operate as international securities depositories. They

---

* They include a number of cental banks and official institutions.

do not hold the securities in custody themselves but rely on a worldwide network of depository banks. The custody services offered by the depositories include storing the issue in the vault, administration of coupon, dividend and redemption payments, related tax services, and the exercise of warrants, conversion and other options. To limit physical movements of securities and enhance security, each individual issue is deposited and immobilised with only one depository; in the case of Euro-bonds this is normally the paying agent for the issue. Typically, the deposited securities become fully fungible, which means that the owner no longer has title to a security with a particular registration number but receives a claim on the pool of securities held by the settlement organisations; the transfer of ownership takes place by book entry in the securities accounts with Euroclear and Cedel.

Apart from custody and settlement services, Euroclear and Cedel offer their customers various other services, including trade matching and confirmation, cash management and financing facilities, proprietary telecommunications systems and securities lending and borrowing programmes. Regarding funds transfer facilities, participants pay and receive funds in the different currencies accepted by the systems through each system's cash correspondent in the respective country of issue.

Settlements procedures

The settlement procedures followed by Euroclear and Cedel are similar and can be summarised in four points. Firstly, both institutions operate a gross securities and cash settlement system: each instruction is carried out individually with the crediting/debiting of securities accounts taking place simultaneously with the corresponding debiting/crediting of the cash accounts. However, the instructions are not carried out on a continuous basis but are stored by the computer up to a certain cut-off time, after which they enter an automated batch settlement programme. All validated and matched settlement instructions enter the settlement process, which is carried out during the night prior to the settlement date.*

Secondly, securities transfers and the related payments are executed on a delivery against payment principle. This means that the settlement of individual transactions is successfully completed only if the selling participant has sufficient securities in his securities account or has access to securities

---

* Until September 1993 Cedel processed, validated and matched instructions in the afternoon on the settlement day. It continues to run a daytime settlement process. Euroclear has announced that it will also introduce a daytime settlement process.

borrowing facilities to permit delivery and if the buyer has a sufficient cash or cash credit position available for payment. Once the settlement programme is terminated, settlement is final and participants are notified of their securities and cash positions. The strict application of the principle means that a number of instructions entering the automated settlement process are not executed. They normally re-enter the settlement process on the following business day.

Thirdly, delivery instructions are not processed in the chronological order in which they are transmitted by the participants but according to a certain rank for each individual issue. The ranking criteria differ between Euroclear and Cedel but include the priority codes given by the participants themselves, the settlement date (normally old instructions before more recent ones) and the nominal amount of the transaction. The automated settlement process groups all trades related to the same issue and subsequently attempts to settle as many trades as possible for each issue using a so called 'chaining' procedure. Very often settlement instructions reflect the fact that the same security has been bought and sold through one or more intermediaries (brokers) a number of times during the trading day. The computer program will, for instance, try to recognise so-called back-to-back transactions involving the purchase and sale by two participants of the same security through a broker and treat such transactions as a group for settlement purposes. The chaining program also tries to settle as many transactions as possible related to the same security in light of the cash and security positions available in the participants' accounts and by taking account of the expected movements in the accounts during the settlement processing style. These patterns of settlement are optimised by recourse to recursive simulations.

Fourthly, since many trades in the international securities market will be conducted by counterparties belonging to the other settlement system, Euroclear and Cedel have automated the linkage between their securities settlements by installing an electronic 'bridge'. Cross-system settlement is thus also handled by book-entry transfers between the two systems. For this, each system maintains a securities and a cash account with the other. When one of the two organisations finds itself with a substantial custody holding for the other, the two systems transfer securities from one system's depository to the other system's depository. In contrast, cash settlements between the two systems take place on a net basis for each individual currency each day. Given that the volume of securities between the two systems results in substantial cash movements as well, each system has arranged a special credit line for the other to cover the inter-system credit exposures.

In order to enable participants to settle transactions in domestic markets through the international settlement systems, Euroclear and Cedel provide two types of linkages to domestic clearing systems. In the case of direct links, Euroclear and Cedel themselves hold an account with a local clearing system and cross-border transactions can be settled without the intervention of the local depository. Where there is no direct link, a local Euroclear/Cedel depository holds an account with its domestic clearing system and trades between Euroclear and Cedel participants and their counterparties in the domestic market are settled through the intermediary of this depository.

Other features (liquidity facilities and risk management)

With respect to risk management in both the Euroclear and the Cedel systems, principal risk is limited by the delivery against payment principle used by both organisations, while liquidity risk is reduced by various cash credit facilities and securities lending programmes. Moreover, the combined exposure for each participant under both these lending schemes must normally be collateralised by holdings of securities (expressed in US dollars). For this, the value of the securities eligible as collateral is marked to market each day and adjustments are made taking into account the type of instrument and the exchange rate of the respective currency of issue vis-à-vis the dollar. With respect to the credit line which Euroclear and Cedel have opened for one another to cover the execution of 'bridge' settlements, this facility is covered by a letter of credit which each system obtains from a separate syndicate of banks.

Central banks are not directly involved in providing payment services for the settlement of international securities transactions. The link with the respective domestic payment systems is through the participation of Euroclear's/Cedel's cash correspondents in the respective local interbank funds transfer systems. Various central banks have a relationship with one or both of the international clearing organisations, however, through the direct or indirect linkage which these systems have with a number of domestic securities settlement systems. For example, Euroclear and Cedel have links with the Banque de France for the settlement of transactions in various domestic government securities, with the Bank of England (for ECU treasury bills), the Nederlandsche Bank (for Euro-commercial paper) and with the National Bank of Belgium.

APPENDIX 5

REAL TIME GROSS SETTLEMENT (RTGS) VIA CONTINUOUS LINKED SETTLEMENT (CLS)

One way to reduce settlement risk has been the use of 'netting' in all its various forms - bilateral via systems like Citinet, multilateral like ECHO or Multinet. Following the Allsopp Report (March 1996) requiring:

- action by individual banks to control their FX settlement exposures,
- collective industry action to provide multi-currency services to reduce risk,
- action by central banks to support and encourage private sector progress,

the subsequent action by the Group of 20 (G20) in investigating the optimum way of reducing risk led to the establishment of CLS Services (CLSS) after the feasibility of running continuous linked settlement was approved. In December 1997 CLSS acquired the share capital of both ECHO and the Multinet International Bank and, at September 1998, there were 60 shareholders from 14 countries.

| Payment (across CLS bank's accounts with central banks) | Members pay the CLS bank in their short currencies |
| | Members receive payment from the CLS bank in their long currencies |

↓ ↑

| Settlement (across members' accounts on CLS bank books) | CLS bank
• posts incoming funds from members
• settles transactions
• pays out settlement proceeds to members |

A pay-in schedule for a settlement bank:

	Net position	Payment due by CET (cumulative amount)				
		8:00	9:00	10:00	11:00	12:00
USD	+100					
EUR	−500	100	200	300	400	500
JPY	−1,000	250	500	750	1,000	
GBP	+300					
CHF	−1,000	200	400	600	800	1,000
CAD	+300					

The CLS bank will have settlement with funding through automated systems:

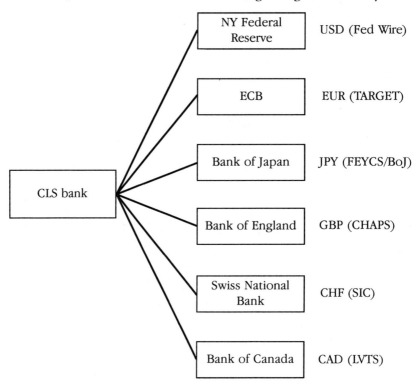

The following diagram shows the interrelationship of all participants in continuous linked settlement:

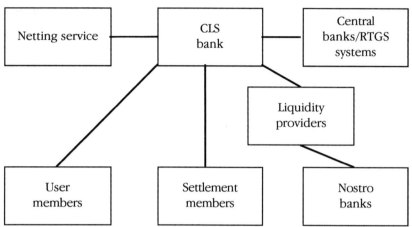

An example of how 'maximum partial settlement' works:

	Member X				**Member Y**			
	Payment due	Cash balance	Limit	Amount payable	Payment due	Cash balance	Limit	Amount payable
USD	100	200	−500	100				
EUR					120	500	−500	120
JPY	100	−300	−300	0				
GBP					100	0	−300	100
CHF	100	−250	−3000	50				
CAD					100	200	−200	100
Total	**300**			**150**	**320**			**320**

Member X can only make payments up to 150, whereas Member Y can make payments up to the full amount payable.

Service suspended since 15 May 1999 and only forecast to recommence in second half of year 2000 with full operation of RTGS.

APPENDIX 6

REPO SETTLEMENTS

Sell/buy back

Example 1
The repo:

Trade date	8 November 1996
Settlement date	12 November 1996
Maturity date	12 December 1996
Term	30 days
Repo rate	5.25% pa (Actual/360)

The collateral:

The bond	GEC 7.00 5/99
Maturity	4 May 1999
On settlement date	188 days' interest accrued
Clean price	102.25
Accrued interest	$\dfrac{188}{360} \times 7.00 = 3.6556$
Dirty price	$102.25 + 3.6556 = 105.9056$

Example 2
The repo:

Trade date	8 November 1996
Settlement date	12 November 1996
Maturity date	12 December 1996
Term	30 days
Repo rate	5.25% pa (Actual/360)

The collateral:

The bond	GEC 5.50 12/98
Maturity	11 December 1998
On settlement date	359 days' interest accrued
Clean price	99.50
Accrued interest	$\frac{359}{360}$ x 5.50 = 5.4847
Dirty price	99.50 + 5.4847 = 104.9847

Example 3

A dealer sells USD 1,000,000 of T-bonds for 7 days. The bonds have 273 days of accrued interest due on spot date, and current market clean price is 100.28. The settlement amount is therefore the full 'dirty' price of the bond:

Clean amount	USD	1,002,800.00
Accrued interest (273/360 x 6.5% x 1 mio)	USD	49,292.67
Settlement amount (dirty price)	USD	1,052,091.67

The repurchase amount depends on the agreed repo rate of interest. If we suppose it was 5.0625%, the interest paid on the dirty amount is thus:

Repo interest (5.0625% x 7/360 x 1,052,091.67)	USD	1,035.65
Investor thus pays in total 1,052,091.67+1,035.65	USD	1,053,127.32

The forward repurchase price then has to be adjusted for the difference between the repo interest due and the accrued interest over the period:

Repo interest (5.0625 x 7/360)	USD	1,035.65
Less accrued (6.5% x 7/360)	USD	1,263.89
Difference (on USD 1 mio nominal)		-228.24

Expressed per USD 100 nominal = -0.022824 (USD)
Thus the repurchase price becomes 100.28 - 0.022824 = 100.257176

Another way to calculate this is:

Investor (buyer) repays	USD	1,053,127.32
after allowing for accrued interest and interest		
on that (49,291.67 + 1,263.89)	USD	50,555.56
	USD	1,002,571.76

ie, a 'price' of 100.257176

Classic repo

Example I - without margin requirement

Settlement date

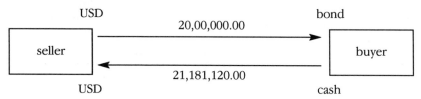

at a dirty price of 105.9056

Maturity date

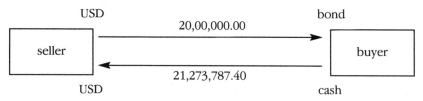

Calculation of repo interest:

$$\frac{21,181,120.00 \times 5.25 \times 30}{360 \times 100} = 92,667.40$$

Total amount to be paid at maturity:
21,181,200.00 + 92,667.40 = 21,273,787.40

With margin requirement (haircut) of 2%
The process would be the same except that the cash amount would be worked out on a bond price that would be calculated as follows:

$$\frac{105.9056 \times 100}{102.00} = 103.8290196$$

This would produce a cash amount of:

$$\frac{103.8290196 \times 20,000,000.00}{100.00} = 20,765,803.92$$

The repo would be calculated in the same way.

Example 2 - with a margin requirement (haircut) of 2% and a margin call

Settlement date

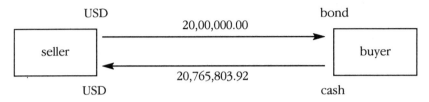

<table>
<tr><td>USD</td><td></td><td>bond</td></tr>
<tr><td>seller</td><td>20,00,000.00 →</td><td>buyer</td></tr>
<tr><td></td><td>← 20,765,803.92</td><td></td></tr>
<tr><td>USD</td><td></td><td>cash</td></tr>
</table>

At a price of $\dfrac{105.9056 \times 100}{102} = 103.8290196$

Maturity date

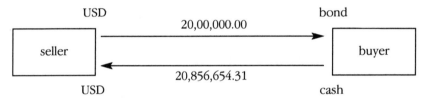

<table>
<tr><td>USD</td><td></td><td>bond</td></tr>
<tr><td>seller</td><td>20,00,000.00 →</td><td>buyer</td></tr>
<tr><td></td><td>← 20,856,654.31</td><td></td></tr>
<tr><td>USD</td><td></td><td>cash</td></tr>
</table>

Calculation of repo interest:

$$\frac{20,765,803.92 \times 5.25 \times 30}{360 \times 100} = 90,850.39$$

Total amount to be paid at maturity:

$$20,765,803.92 + 90,850.39 = 20,856.654.31$$

If, on 18 November 1996, the price of the bond fell to 100.50 then the amount of the security would have to be recalculated as follows:

Clean price: 100.5000
Accrued interest: $\dfrac{194 \times 7,00}{360.00} = 3.7722222$
Dirty price: 104.2722
Impact of haircut: $\dfrac{104.2722222 \times 100}{102.00} = 102.2276688$

Required security: original cash amount = $\dfrac{20{,}765{,}803.92 \times 100}{102.2276688}$

= 20,313,291.07

If the bond is available in amount of USD 1,00.00 then the seller would have to put up additional collateral of USD 314,000.00.

The relevant transfers that would subsequently take place are as follows:

18 November 1996 - settlement date

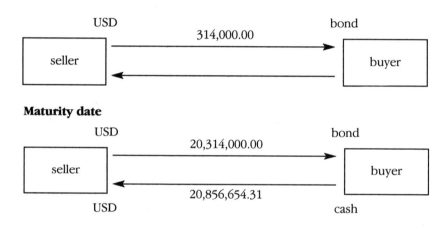

Maturity date

149

APPENDIX 7

THE KEY ATTRACTIONS OF CHAPS EURO

The CHAPS board is raising the profile of the CHAPS euro system and actively marketing the service which it will provide. Copies are available by e-mail from: sm.chapseuro@apacs.org.uk. The CHAPS board is now drawing attention to the fact that CHAPS euro is based on the same concept as, and will sit alongside, the present CHAPS sterling service which is widely understood and appreciated.

The CHAPS Company's aim is to provide a euro service at least as good as the CHAPS sterling service. CHAPS euro's twin purposes are:

- To be a stand-alone real time gross settlement (RTGS) system based in London.
- To be the UK's access route to TARGET.

Because of the scale of euro activity expected to take place in UK financial markets, the stand-alone role of CHAPS euro will be very important.

The major attractive features of CHAPS euro are as follows:

- *It is a riskless system:* As with CHAPS sterling, CHAPS euro will be a true RTGS system, with each payment settled immediately in real-time at the Bank of England. So intraday finality is provided and settlement risk eliminated.

- *CHAPS has a proven capacity to undertake major developments:* In total, the CHAPS Company has a 14-year track record of providing a high quality payment service combined with a robust system. In 1996, the CHAPS Company, in partnership with the Bank of England, transformed the UK sterling wholesale payment system from an end-of-day net settlement system to an RTGS system. This project was successfully completed on schedule, without in any way affecting end-users or causing any diminution to the service provided. The development of a parallel euro system is, by comparison, relatively straightforward.

- *Resilient and robust in handling high volumes:* The CHAPS sterling RTGS system has been resilient and robust, operating without hitch since its inception over two years ago. It is the largest RTGS system in Europe, and second in the world only to Fedwire in the USA. On a peak day CHAPS has handled 135,000 payments with a value of £240 billion. Although CHAPS euro is being planned on the basis of initial traffic considerably lower than for CHAPS sterling, the RTGS processor will be capable of handling whatever volumes are required, without reducing the efficiency of the service, by adding capacity.

- *Broad geographic coverage:* The CHAPS euro system includes a database showing all the CHAPS euro addressable bank identifier codes (BICs). Ultimately there are likely to be 20,000 BICs, including both UK and foreign bank addresses. Any bank will thus be able to use the database to route payments automatically to a wide range of destinations using straight-through processing, with an excellent level of recipient bank service.

- *Easy access via SWIFT:* Rather than using a proprietary system, CHAPS euro is based on the SWIFT Fin Copy product, which enables low cost connections to the service to be made from anywhere in the world. So CHAPS euro will combine the experience, quality and resilience of CHAPS sterling with the ease of access of SWIFT.

- *Fast and efficient:* CHAPS works as a high-speed system with minimal delays to payments. Once a sending bank releases a payment, the average time taken for it to reach a receiving bank is less than one minute, which compares favourably with any other European payment system. This is of great value to banks and their customers for time-critical payments.

- *Liquidity efficiency:* As with CHAPS sterling, the CHAPS euro system has been designed to ensure liquidity efficiency, which is achieved through careful liquidity management and scheduling of payments by members. CHAPS uses the minimum liquidity necessary to ensure that payments experience little or no delay awaiting capacity. This allows CHAPS members to provide their customers with a highly efficient service.

- *Well understood operational rules:* The CHAPS community has sound and well understood operational rules. Service level agreements ensure discipline in the CHAPS system whilst at the same time providing that member performance does not impact adversely on end-user customers. A smooth flow of payments is brought about by guidelines on members which determine payment volumes through the system at various points during the day. Under CHAPS' end-to-end service levels and agreements, a sending member knows the service level it offers to customers. Customers must be credited on a same-day basis by recipient banks. The full amount of each payment is always credited to the customer's account.

- *Open all hours:* The CHAPS Board has confirmed that CHAPS euro will be open on every day that TARGET is open (ie, every weekday except Christmas Day and New Year's Day; when Christmas Day and New Year's Day fall on a weekend, there is to be no holiday in lieu) and for the full operating hours each day (ie, 07.00 to 18.00 CET for banks and 07.00 to 17.00 CET for customers).

- *Competitive in price:* CHAPS euro will be priced competitively against other major euro payment systems. As it has a large database of automatically-addressable banks, there will be significantly reduced manual intervention. As a result, the overall cost of settling CHAPS euro will be less than for systems with fewer members and participants.

- *CHAPS is managed by banks taking into account their commercial needs:* CHAPS is a member-owned and directed system which allows it to develop in ways which its members wish, in order to meet their needs. Members control their own payment flow in CHAPS. It will not be compulsory to schedule payments within CHAPS euro, and the decision about how and when to make payments is within members' control rather than decided by any third party. Sending banks know precisely where payments are in the end-to-end process at all times, and each member knows the position of its settlement account at the Bank of England through on-line links. Tried and trusted procedures are also in place to avoid members' balances falling below zero at the end of the day.

- *Operational and technical support:* CHAPS provides its members with a full range of operational and technical support, including support in contingency situations and a rapid response to any problems which might arise.

- *Fully tested, giving absolute confidence in CHAPS euro's reliability:* The CHAPS euro system is currently undergoing a comprehensive testing programme which offers a strong degree of confidence in its availability, reliability, and integrity in the euro environment. All members have participated in group testing within CHAPS euro, and the Bank of England has sent payment messages across TARGET Interlinking to central banks in other countries. Integrated systems testing of all components of CHAPS euro and the linkages to TARGET, including central bank systems, is now in progress. Volume and performance testing is taking place to test both the resilience of the system to Year 2000 issues and each member knows the position of its settlement account at the Bank of England through on-line links. Tried and trusted procedures are also in place to avoid members' balances falling below zero at the end of the day.

APPENDIX 8

EURO FACILITIES AT THE FIRST CHICAGO CLEARING CENTRE (FCCC)

In preparation for the introduction of the euro, the First Chicago Clearing Centre (FCCC) now provides issuing and paying agency (IPA) services for euro-denominated certificates of deposit (CDs). The aim of this new service is to provide an operational framework to support the development of the euro money market in London. The number of players, the size of the market and the quality of service providers and settlement infrastructures will make London a leading centre for the euro money markets.

Background

FCCC provides IPA clearing and settlement services for London money market instruments, most of which are currently denominated in US dollars or sterling. All dollar CDs are issued in physical form but, since 1994, most sterling CDs have been issued in dematerialised form into the central money markets office (CMO). Clearing and settlement of these instruments can take place within FCCC, which offers book-entry delivery versus payment (DVP) settlement. Some dollar CDs settle physically; most sterling CDs settle in the CMO. Euroclear is a participant in FCCC, allowing CDs to settle with Euroclear same day. FCCC is a recognised clearing system and is regulated by the FSA.

Form of physical euro CDs

FCCC will provide issuers with euro-denominated CDs in standard definitive format using generic blank certificates. They are preprinted with the euro symbol, denomination and the note number. When issued, FCCC prints the issuer's name and pre-agreed wording on the blank CD. These CDs carry all necessary security features required for 'London Good Delivery'.

Settlement

Primary CD issuance in FCCC

Settlement at issuance of a euro-denominated CD before 1 January 1999 will be against ECU. At maturity, or on interest payment dates after 1 January 1999, the issuer will pay in euros. Euro-denominated CDs will be expected to have a maturity date beyond 1 January 1999.

Secondary market settlement in FCCC

Secondary market trades will settle on a DVP basis over an ECU account in FCCC before 1 January 1999 and over a euro account after that date. FCCC will automatically convert ECU accounts to euro accounts over the conversion weekend, both for cash and securities, on a 1:1 basis.

ICSDs

Euro CDs will be eligible for settlement in Euroclear and Cedel Bank via the direct specialised depository link between Euroclear and FCCC.

Euro CMO

FCCC will also be an inaugural member of the euro CMO, which went live on 4 January 1999. From that date onwards, euro-denominated CDs can also be issued in dematerialised form and existing euro-denominated CDs can be lodged in the CMO.

Conclusion

FCCC's soundings suggest that there is a considerable interest in issuing and trading euro-denominated CDs in London. The services offered by FCCC and the euro CMO will enable institutions fully to meet this demand.

APPENDIX 9

EURO SCHEDULE

Planned timetable for the introduction of the euro in first-wave member states

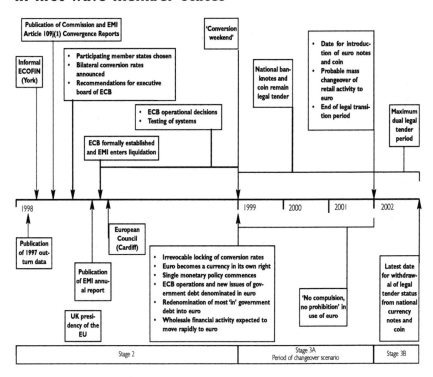

APPENDIX 10

MAJOR ISO TRADING CURRENCY CODES

AUD	Australian dollars
ATS	Austrian schillings
BEF	Belgian francs
CAD	Canadian dollars
CHF	Swiss francs
DEM	German marks
DKK	Danish krone
ESP	Spanish pesetas
EUR	Euro
FMK	Finish marks
FRF	French francs
GBP	Great Britain pounds
HKD	Hong Kong dollars

Major ISO trading currency codes

IEP	Irish punts
JPY	Japanese yen
MYR	Malayan ringgitts
NLG	Netherland guilders
NOK	Norwegian kroner
NTD	New Taiwanese dollars
NZD	New Zealand dollars
PTE	Portuguese escudos
SAR	Saudi Arabian riyal
SEK	Swedish krona
USD	US dollars

APPENDIX 11

FORMULAE

Money markets

The **simple interest** formula is: $\dfrac{P \times R \times T}{100 \times Base}$

where:

I	=	Interest
P	=	Principal
R	=	Rate
T	=	Time (number of days)

The **discount formula** is:

$$Proceeds = FV - \left[FV \left(\frac{T \times DR}{B \times 100} \right) \right]$$

$$= 1{,}000{,}000 - \left[1{,}000{,}000 \left(\frac{90 \times 10}{36500} \right) \right]$$

$$= 1{,}000{,}000 - 24{,}657.53 = 975{,}342.47$$

where:

FV	=	Face value
T	=	Time
DR	=	Discount rate
B	=	Base (360 or 365 days)

The **true yield** is:

$$\text{True yield} = \frac{\text{Discount rate}}{\left[1 - \left(\dfrac{\text{Discount rate x T}}{\text{Base x 100}} \right) \right]}$$

Formula for forward/forward or FRAs

The formula for forward/forward interest rate or FRAs as is commonly known:

$$\left[\frac{(R_L \text{ x } D_L) - (R_S \text{ x } D_S)}{(D_L \text{ x } D_S) \text{ x } \left[1 + \dfrac{(R_S \text{ x } D_S)}{(B \text{ x } 100)} \right]} \right]$$

RL	=	Rate from start date to the far date (long period)
DL	=	Number of days from spot to the far date
RS	=	Rate from spot to the near date (short period)
DS	=	Number of days from spot to the near date
B	=	Day basis (360 or 365)

NB Some currencies are quoted from same day value, eg, GBP.

The FRA settlement formula is:

$$\left[\frac{(L - R) \text{ or } (R - L) \text{ x } D \text{ x } A}{(D \text{ x } L) + (B \text{ x } 100)} \right]$$

L	=	Libor (BBA settlement rate)
R	=	Contract reference rate
A	=	Contract amount
D	=	Days in contract period
B	=	Day basis (360 or 365)

The present value over several periods is:

$$\text{Present value} = \frac{\text{Future value in Year 'n'}}{(1 + r)\, n}$$

Where 'r' is interest/discount rate applying (expressed as a decimal - ie, 10% = 0.10) and 'n' is the number of years. Therefore, if the discount rate is 10% and FV is £100 then today £100 is worth £100/1.10 = £90.91 : £100 FV in two years is £100/1.21 = £82.64, etc.

The semi-annual to annual rate of 6.86% must be annualised using the following conversion formula:

$$[(1+ \frac{6.86}{200})2\text{-}1] \times 100 = 6.9776$$

To convert the annual rate of 7.45% to a semi-annual equivalent use the following conversion formula:

$$\left[\sqrt{\frac{1+7.45}{100}} \right] 1 \times 200 = 7.3161$$

Options

Delta
The delta of an option measures the change in the price of an option relative to the change in the price of the underlying thus:

$$\text{Delta} \quad = \quad \frac{\text{change in price of option}}{\text{change in price of underlying}}$$

Thus if USD/DEM changes from 1.82 to 1.78, an option price by 2 US cents, then the delta is expressed as 2/4 = 0.5.

Deltas can never change more than the change in the underlying, also the cost of the option cannot move in the opposite direction to the change in the underlying, thus the maximum range of delta is 0 to 1.

An option close to maturity which is in-the-money will thus have a delta which tends towards 1, while one that is out-of-the-money will tend towards zero.

Gamma
The gamma of an option measure the change in the delta compared to the change in the underlying and is expressed thus:

Formulae

$$\text{Gamma} = \frac{\text{change in delta}}{\text{change in underlying}}$$

Thus, if delta for USD/DEM option moves from 0.5 to 0.6, and the underlying from 1.82 to 1.78, then gamma = 0.1/4 = 0.25.

Gamma is highest when the option is near to maturity and close to being at-the-money. Gamma tends to zero for deep in-the-money or deep out-of-the-money options.

Gamma is often used in constructing a position that would benefit from high volatility. This would be the purchase of a straddle where you buy a call and put at the same strike, so that - provided the option price does change enough in either direction - there will be a profit on either the call or the put which will exceed the loss on the other option which would be limited to the premium paid.

Theta
The theta of an option measures the change in the options price to the decrease in time to expiry. The value of an option decreases as time goes by - time decay - and thus the theta of an option has to be negative, so that an option with a theta of 0.025% would lose USD 250 per day on a nominal value of USD 1,000,000.

Theta is highest when options are at the money (ATM) and it is less susceptible to changes at the beginning of the period but decays rapidly towards expiry.

Vega or kappa
The vega monitors the change in the option's price relative to changes in volatility. Thus were volatility to increase 1% and the premium increased by USD 2,500, then the vega would be quoted as 0.25% on a face value of an option of USD 1,000,000.

Vega is highest when options are ATM and are a bigger influence on the price of the option the longer the maturity.

Rho
The rho measures the change in the price compared to the change in interest rates. Even if the spot price does not change, since the forward price is based on interest rate differentials, then a move in either interest rate will affect the price of the option. However, since we are only concerned

with the difference between the two rates, rho is the least influential of factors in options pricing. Thus, if the differential moves by 1% and price by USD 1.25 then its rho is +1.25.

Calculating payment under cap

$$\frac{(\text{Libor} - \text{strike rate}) \times \text{days} \times \text{notional amount}}{\text{Days basis} \times 100}$$

Calculating payment on floor

$$\frac{(\text{Strike rate} - \text{Libor}) \times \text{days} \times \text{notional amount}}{\text{Days basis} \times 100}$$

APPENDIX 12

CALENDAR BASIS

The alternative calendar conventions for calculating day count and annual basis are as follows:

Actual/actual: This means the day count is the actual number of days in the period but the annual basis is the number of days in current coupon x number of coupons per annum which means that coupon payments are always equal amounts.

Actual/365 (A/365): The annual basis is 365 days and the day count is the actual number of days in the period.

30E/360: The annual basis is 360 days and it is assumed that there is never more or less than 30 days in the day count for a complete month.

30/360: This is similar to the 30E/360 days in that there is assumed to be never more than 30 days in the day count for a month.

The difference between the 30E/360 and 30/360 convention can be shown by the following table:

Number of days of interest accrued from 1 July			
To	**30 July**	**31 July**	**1 August**
30E/360	29	29	30
30/360	29	30	30

Actual/360 (A/360): The annual basis is 360 days and the day count is the actual number of days in the period.

Actual/actual: The annual basis for semi-annual bonds is *twice* the actual number of days in the current semi-annual coupon period. The day count is the actual number of days in the period.

APPENDIX 13

OPERATIONAL RISK ACCORDING TO GENERALLY ACCEPTED REPORTING PROCEDURE (GARP)

Transaction risk

Execution error
       Product complexity
       Booking error
       Settlement error
       Commodity delivery risk
       Documentary/contract risk

Operational control risk

Exceeding limit
       Rogue trading
       Fraud
       Money laundering
       Security risk
       Key personnel risk
       Processing risk

Systems risk

Programming error
       Model/methodology error
       Market-to-market error
       Management information
       IT systems failure
       Telecommunications failure
       Contingency planning

Business events risk

       Currency convertibility risk
       Shift in credit rating
       Reputation risk
       Taxation risk
       Legal risk
       Disaster risk
       Natural disasters
       Wars
       Collapse/suspension of market

Regulatory risk

       Breaching capital requirements
       Regulatory changes

FUTURES CONTRACTS: EXAMPLES ON THE LONDON INTERNATIONAL FINANCIAL FUTURES EXCHANGE (LIFFE)

Futures

Short-term interest rate

Three-month sterling
Three-month Euroswiss
Three-month euro
Three-month Euroyen

Government bonds

Long gilt
Japanese government bond (JGB)

UK stock indices

FT-SE 100 (Financial Times Stock Exchange)
FT-SE mid-250

Options

Options on short-term interest rate futures

Three-month sterling
Three-month Euroswiss

Options on government bond futures

Long gilt

UK stock index options

FT-SE 100 (American-style exercise)
FT-SE 100 (European-style exercise)
FT-SE 100 FLEX

Appendix 15

London Code of Conduct: SUMMARY OF SECTIONS

APPENDIX 16

USEFUL ADDRESSES

APACS
Mercury House
Triton Court
14 Finsbury Square
London FC2A I BR
Tel: 0171 711 6234
Website: www.apacs.org.uk

BACS Limited
3 De Havilland Road
Edgware
Middlesex HA8 SQA
Tel: 0181 9522333
Fax: 0181 951 7480

CHAPS
(address as for APACS)
Tel: 0171 711 6356
Fax: 0171 3829783

The Bank of England
Policy/editorial
Threadneedle Street
London EC2R 8AH
Tel: 0171 601 4300
Fax: 0171 601 4830

Useful addresses

Banking and Market Services
(address as above)
Tel: 0171 601 4685
Fax: 0171 601 3133

and
Tel: 0171 601 3568
Fax: 0171 601 4455

The Bank for International Settlements
Basle
Switzerland
Tel: + 4161 280 8080
Fax: + 4161 280 9100/8100
Website: www.bis.org

Bloomberg LP
City Gate House
39-45 Finsbury Square
London EC2A 1PQ
Tel: 0171 330 7500
Fax: 0171 392 6200

The British Bankers' Association
Pinners Hall
105-108 Old Broad Street
London EC2N lEX
Tel: 0171 216 8862
Fax: 0171 216 8958

The Building Societies' Association
3 Savile Row
London W1X 1AF
Chairman, AD2000 Panel
Tel: 01908 233762

Secretary, AD2000 Panel
Tel: 0171 4402245

Cedel Group
UK:
Floor 42
One Canada Square

Canary Wharf
London E14 5DR

Europe:
67 Boulevard Grande Duchesse Charlotte
L-1331
Luxembourg
Tel: +352 44 99 24 74
Fax: +352 44 99 29 47 4

Website: www.cedelgroup.com

Dow Jones
10 Fleet Place
Limeburner Lane
London EC4M 7QN
Tel: 0171 832 9000
Fax: 0171 832 9924

ECHO (Exchange Clearing House)
Exchange Clearing House Ltd
Exchange Tower
One Harbour Exchange Square
London E14 9GE
Tel: 0171 971 5700
Fax: 0171 971 5729
Website: www.exchangeclearinghouse.co.uk

Euroclear
Boulevard E. Jacqmain 151
B-1210 Brussels
Belgium
Tel: +32 2 224 1211
Fax: +32 2 224 1287

The Financial Services Authority
30-34 Kingsway
London WC2B 6E5
Tel: 0171 663 5374
Fax: 0171 663 5059

The Futures and Options Association

One America Square
17 Crosswall
London EC3N 2PP
Tel: 0171 426 7250
Fax: 0171 426 7251
E-mail: info @foa.co.uk
Website: www.foa.co.uk

The Joint Exchanges Committee

LIFFE Administration and Management
Cannon Bridge
London EC4R 3XX
Tel: 0171 623 0444
Fax: 0171 588 3624

London Metal Exchange
56 Leadenhall Street
London EC3A 2DX
Tel: 0171 264 5522

International Petroleum Exchange
International House
1 St Katherine's Way
London E1 9UN
Tel: 0171 265 5717
Fax: 0171 481 8485
Website: www.ipe.uk.com

The London Clearing House Ltd
Aldgate House
33 Aldgate High Street
London EC3N 1EA
Tel: 0171 426 7042
Fax: 0171 426 7001

The London Stock Exchange

London EC2N 1HP
Tel: 01959 565 8368
Fax: 01959 561 721
Website: www.londonstockexuser.co.uk

Reuters
Europe/UK:
Corporate Headquarters
Reuters Group plc
85 Fleet Street
London EC4P 4AJ
Tel: 0171 250 1122

America :
1700 Broadway
New York
NY 10019
USA
Tel: +1(212) 603 3300

Asia:
10th Floor Citiplaza 3
14 Taikoo Wan Road
Taikoo Sing, Quarry Bay
Hong Kong
Tel: +852 2843 6363

SWIFT
Headquarters:
1 Avenue Adèle
B-1310 La Hulpe
Belgium
Tel: +32 2 655 3111
Fax: +32 2 655 3226

GLOSSARY OF TERMS

ACS: Automated confirmations system which includes BART and TRAM.

Arbitrage: Simultaneous purchase and sale of a currency in two or more markets to take advantage of discrepancies in prices. Spot forward or both. Often now used to mean 'interest arbitrage'.

Assignment of FX contract: A contract between one of the bank's customers and another bank on which you agree to accept your customers' responsibilities under the contract in return for a cash receipt/payment.

BART: Bank's automated reception terminal, ie, the PC at which a bank accesses ACS, etc.

Bid: Price at which a price maker is willing to borrow or purchase a foreign currency.

BIS: The Bank for International Settlements, Basle. The Central Banks' central bank.

Broken dates: Rates quoted for specific dates between recognised dealing period, eg, 1 month and 22 days, which lies between the straight one month and two month maturities.

Cable: The term given to spot GBP/USD, since originally the price went via a cable under the Atlantic.

CAD: The Capital Adequacy Directive of 1996 from BIS.

Call/demand: Short-term funds similar to current accounts which provide immediate funds and attract interest.

Cap: A cap is a loan where the rate is fixed at a maximum level at the outset and will not vary even if market rates go above the level of the cap. Also if the variable rate goes below the cap, the borrower will often get the benefit of a lower rate.

Cedel: Cedel is an institution which settles bonds, etc, on behalf of institutions (see Appendix 4).

Certificate of deposit (CD): A negotiable certificate of deposit is a marketable receipt for funds deposited in a bank for a specified rate of interest. Domestic and euro CDs are issued on a 360-day basis with interest paid at maturity if the instrument has a maturity of one year or less (euro's annual if past one year). Since it is a tradeable security it is usually issued in bearer form.

CGO: Central Gilts Office - based at the Bank of England this is an electronic settlement facility for gilts only (see also CMO).

CHAPS: A UK institution for the settlement of GBP payments (see Appendix 3).

CHIPS: A US based organisation which settles USD payments on behalf of correspondents (see Appendix 3).

CIRS: A currency interest rate swap where more than one currency is involved.

CMO: Central Money Markets Office - based at the Bank of England for all non-gilts GBP settlements (see also CGO).

Collar: A collar sets an upper and lower base for the interest rate on a loan/ investment.

Collateral deposit: A deposit taken as security for a loan, or cover of a letter of credit. It could be either fixed or at call.

Convertibility: A currency can be exchanged for another currency without restrictions irrespective of who owns the money and without having to obtain permission from the authorities.

Cross rate: Normal interpretation is an exchange of one foreign currency for another, other than local currency, ie, in New York, any pair of currencies which does not include USD, eg, EUR/JPY.

Customer daily settlement limit: The maximum cumulative amount in all currencies spot and/or future, to be settled on any single day by a customer. One side only of each transaction shall be included in this calculation.

Customer foreign exchange limit: The maximum cumulative amount (often now the net amount) of dealings spot and/or forward, in any or all currencies that is permitted to be outstanding at any one time in the name of a customer. One side only of each transaction shall be included in this calculation.

Dealing date: The date on which a deal is actually contracted.

Discount: When currency A buys less of currency B at a future date then A is said to be at a discount to B.

EBS: European Broking System - a rival electronic broking system to R-2002.

ECB: The ECB is the new European Central Bank based in Frankfurt which will set policy and rates for all the 11 members of the euro.

Federal funds: Purchase or sale of uncommitted Fed member bank deposits, usually overnight, at a specified Fed funds rate.

Fixed deposit: A deposit taken for a fixed period of time at a fixed rate of interest. Fixed deposits may be repaid prior to maturity but are subject to an interest adjustment based on the cost of replacing the funds to the maturity of the deposit.

Floor: A floor is a guaranteed minimum rate of return on a deposit. Thus the depositor will receive the rate on the floor even if market rates go below its level.

Foreign currency loan: A loan denominated in non-local currencies, which is extended by a bank to a correspondent.

Foreign exchange gap: Gaps are created by mismatched maturities in each currency's forward exchange book. These gaps represent foreign exchange risk.

Foreign exchange swap: The simultaneous purchase (or sale) of an amount of foreign currency against the sale (or purchase) of the same amount of currency for a different date. The following three definitions are special cases of swaps, all related to funding, and distinguished by their purpose.

- *Position swap:* The execution of a foreign exchange swap to close a net foreign exchange position which resulted from making loan and placements and accepting deposits in a variety of currencies without attempting to exactly match.

- *Funding swap general:* The execution of a foreign exchange swap to generate funds in a currency for which there is an anticipated need from funds in a currency which is available or a currency which, together with a swap premium/discount, is attractively priced.

- *Funding swap specific:* The execution of a foreign exchange swap to generate currency to fund a specific asset from deposit funds in another currency and to sell the loan proceeds forward for the deposit currency

Foreign exchange trading: The process of trading a given amount of one national currency for the approximate equivalent value of another currency. Currencies are usually traded with correspondents in spot trades, outright forward trades or swaps.

Forward: A forward contract is a foreign exchange deal made for delivery on any value date in the future. For practical purposes it is defined as a purchase or sale of foreign currencies against sterling or another currency for commercial purposes or cover of principal and interest on foreign currency loans and deposits, to mature at a given date normally over and above seven days. A forward contract is entered into to eliminate any risk of exchange rates moving between the time that a commitment is first established and the date of actual delivery of funds. For example, if one of the bank's customers knows that in three months time he will need dollars for payment of goods imported from the USA he will buy these dollars from the bank now on a forward basis, value date on which the import is required to be settled. This eliminates any risk for him of rate movements between now and three months' time and he knows now what the exchange is in order that he may calculate his costs accordingly. The dealer in turn would normally cover the deal in the market.

> *Option exchange contract:* A contract for foreign exchange with an optional settlement date. In this type of contract, a period of time is stated during which the person who has the option can choose any day for liquidation and settlement of the contract. The contract will state which party has the option and is usually employed when the date on which foreign exchange will be needed or will be available is not known. These options *must* be carried out by the final date of the contract.

FRA: An FRA is defined as a forward rate agreement between any two banks seeking to protect themselves against a future interest movement in interest rates. The two parties involved agree an interest rate for a specified period of time, from a specified future settlement date (minimum period one month) based on an agreed principal amount.

FSA: The Financial Services Authority is a new regulatory body in the UK which eventually will assume responsibility for control of all markets in the UK - FX, MM, insurance etc.

Funding gap: Gaps created by mismatched maturities in each individual currency's asset and liability portfolio. These gaps represent interest rate risk.

Futures: These represent a firm commitment to buy or sell a specific commodity, during a specified month at a price established through open auction or outcry in a central regulated market place.

Hedging: Hedging is carried out to reduce risk on known future exposures whether in the FX or money markets.

IRS: An IRS is an interest rate swap - a means of changing the interest flows from fixed to floating or vice versa.

Libor: London Inter Bank Offered Rate. Each day at 11 am a group of bankers declare their offered rates for the traditional fixed periods, ie, 1, 2, 3 or 6 months. The mean rate is thus established as the Libor fixing or basis for all commercial loan agreements and FRABBA terms (see Appendix 2) for off-balance sheet trading instruments.

Glossary of terms

LIFFE: The London International Financial Futures Exchange - it was an all 'open outcry' market for the trading of financial futures and options but is now heavily mechanised to screen trading.

Line of credit: An obligation to extend short-term credit to a correspondent, subject to periodic review, amendment or cancellation at any time.

Long: Long in a currency means overbought spot, forward or in total.

MLRO: A money laundering reporting officer, who is required, under Bank of England requirements, to report any suspicion that the source of funds may be from illegal sources, eg, drugs.

Money market investments: These provide correspondents with ways to cover their temporary cash surpluses into short-term earnings assets through highly liquid instruments.

NCB: An NCB is the term applied to the National Central Bank of a member country of the euro as opposed to the ECB or European Central Bank.

NDFs: Non-deliverable forwards - a system for trading in exotic currencies where forwards would normally be restricted or unavailable.

Nostro: Your nostro account is an account in a foreign currency where you take delivery of that currency.

Off-balance sheet items: These instruments, unlike cash, do not cause money to change hands upon their purchase or sale and therefore do not represent assets when owned. They are contingent liabilities which bind the owner to some future action.

Offer: The rate at which a price maker is willing to either lend or sell a foreign currency.

Options: A buyer is granted the right (but not the obligation) to buy or sell financial instruments at standard prices and times in the future.

Outright: Merely the second half of a swap, but made up of the spot rate plus or minus the forward points.

Overdraft loan: Short-term loan extended by the bank to a correspondent to fulfil unexpected funding requirements.

Pips*:* Pip or point in a foreign exchange quotation is literally the last digit in a foreign exchange quotation (normally the fourth place to right of decimal). If one sterling GBP equals 1.5501 USD, then one pip is 0.0001 of a dollar.

Premium: When currency A buys more of currency B at a future date then A is said to be at a premium to B.

Prime rate: The minimum interest rate that banks charge their biggest, best and most creditworthy corporate customers. It is a base on which to scale all interest rates.

Repurchase agreements: Contracts involving the sale of government and agency securities with commitment to repurchase at a future date at the same price plus a stipulated interest charge. The USA had the first market, but repurchase agreements now exist in most developed bond markets (Germany, UK, France, Italy, etc). There are two types - 'sell/buy back' and 'classic'. Settlements for both are described in detail in Appendix 6.

Reverse repurchase agreements: Contracts involving the purchase of securities with commitment to return them at a future date for the original price plus interest.

Revolving credit: A formal commitment allowing a correspondent to borrow and repay loans at will under specific terms and conditions.

Rollover: Banks are typically borrowers of short-term funds but lenders of long-term funds, consequently they are vulnerable to upward movements in interest rates which would increase the cost of their own borrowings but not necessarily that of their loans. Therefore they vary terms of their loans at regular intervals to reflect changes in the cost of funds.

RTGS: Real time gross settlement is the name given to the most recent 'system' to ensure 'finality of payment', ie, a system that will ensure that both parties receive simultaneously the amounts due to them, thereby guaranteeing that a Herstatt situation cannot arise.

Short: Short in a currency means oversold spot, forward or in total.

Spot: The purchase or sale of foreign currencies which normally must be received or delivered within a period of time not exceeding two business days. Occasionally, purchases or sales of foreign currencies are made for delivery three and five business days after the dealing date, to allow for weekends and/or holidays. Some countries practise delivery after three to five days anyway and still call this 'spot'.

Spread: The point/interest rate difference between the bid and offer price.

SRO: Self-regulating organisation, eg, LAUTRO for life assurance. All SROs will come together under the Financial Services Authority (FSA).

SSIs: Standard settlement instructions which are exchanged between counterparts to specify the agent (nostro) where they will always take delivery of a specific currency.

Swap cost and swap income: In funding swap transactions, the differences between the spot and forward rates is regarded as an interest factor called the swap cost or swap income.

SWIFT: Society for Worldwide International Financial Telecommunications, the prime agent in Europe for the settlement of foreign currency transactions.

TARGET: The name of the settlement system for the euro.

Term loan: The formal commitment with a final maturity usually in excess of one year, in which a correspondent repays according to a formal agreement.

TRAM: Transaction automatic matching - part of the ACS - for the automatic matching of confirmations.

TRAX: The system into which all bond transactions have to be entered within 30 minutes of execution to allow confirmation to take place.

Triangulation: The term given to the method of working out the countervalue of two 'in' currencies against each other via their rates against the euro.

Value date: The date on which the transaction is to be settled (delivery or receipt of funds).

VaR: Value at risk, the most recent development in assessing the market risk of an institution's complete exposure. The three main methods are co-variance, historical and Monte Carlo.

Vostro: A vostro account is the account held by another bank at your bank, eg, GBP account held by Deutsche Bank with your bank in London.

Yard: A slang term for 1,000 million (an American billion) of a currency. Now only usually used for JPY.

BIBLIOGRAPHY

General
The Foreign Exchange and Money Markets Guide, Julian Warmsley, Wiley, 1992.

Options
Foreign Exchange Options, Alan Hicks, Woodhead Publishing, 1993.

Mastering Foreign Exchange and Currency Options, Francesca Taylor, FT Pitman, 1997.

Derivatives - general
Mastering Derivatives Markets, Francesca Taylor, FT Pitman, 1996.

Swaps
Swaps Workbook 1 (interest rate swaps), *International Financing Review*, £35 from IFR. (Also available in Japanese from IFR.)

Swap Workbook 2 (currency swaps), *International Financing Review*, £35 from IFR. (Also available in the US from Probus Publishing.)

Futures
An Introduction, LIFFE. Free from LIFFE in brochure format.

Short-Term Interest Rate Futures and Options: An Introduction to Strategic Examples, LIFFE. Free from LIFFE in brochure format.

Bibliography

Gilts
The Market in Gilt-Edged Securities and Annual Reviews, Bank of England. Free from the Bank of England.

Money Markets
Introduction to International Repo', Garban Securities. Free brochure available from Harlow Butler Broking or Garban Securities in most major centres.

The Money Market, 3rd edition, Marcia Stigum, Dow Jones-Irwin, 1990 .

Regulations
London Code of Conduct, Bank of England. Free from the Bank of England.

The ACI Code of Conduct, ACI. Free to members of the ACI and FFR 75 to non-members.

The Tokyo Code of Conduct, ACI. Free to members of the ACI and FFR 75 to non-members

The New York Code of Conduct, ACI. Free to members of the ACI and FFR 75 to non-members

The Singapore Code of Conduct, ACI. Free to members of the ACI and FFR 75 to non-members

Financial Services Authority: an outline, The Financial Services Authority, May 1998

Technical Analysis
Technical Analysis of the Futures Markets, John J. Murphy, New York Institute of Finance, 1986.

Repo
NatWest Markets Handbook of International Repo, Daniel Corrigan, Christopher Georgiou, Jonathan Gollow.

Mastering Repo Markets, Robert Steiner, FT Pitman, 1997.

Real Time Gross Settlement
BIS report Basle 1997

VaR

Riskmetrics, J.P Morgan.

Value at Risk, special supplement June 1996 to *Risk Magazine.*

EMU and the euro

Practical Issues arising from the Introduction of the Euro - periodically issued free by the Bank of England.

Systemic risk

Global Institutions, National Supervision and Systemic Risk, G-30 publication, 1997.

Risks (derivatives)

Risk Management Guidelines for Derivatives, BIS 1994.

Analysing Sumitomo, Mari Kooi, published in *Swiss Commodities,* November 1996.

Not Just One Man, Lilian Chew.

Risk - operational

Report of the Board of Banking Supervision Inquiry into the collapse of Barings, Bank of England, 1995.

The Year 2000: A Challenge for Financial Institutions and Bank Supervisors, Basle Committee on Banking Supervision, 1997.

Financial Institutions Reform, Recovery and Enforcement Act (FIRREA), 1989.

Report on Netting Schemes (The Angell Report), 1989

Consultative paper on on-balance sheet netting, BIS 1998.

The Lamfalussy Standards, BIS 1990.

INDEX

Index